DAHIJ

Felwine Sarr

DAHIJ

Translated from the French
by Victor Reinking

Peregrine Press

Published by Peregrine Press
4124 39th Avenue SW
Seattle, Washington 98116
peregrinepress.us

ISBN: 979-8-9948941-0-1

Printed in the United States of America

Cover Design by PAR Studio

To Doudou Kaolack and Rokhy Adama,
who entrusted me to the light of their days
To Sarah, Gnilane, Fakhane
To Majnun, to Marie

Contents

The Text and Other Texts

This morning I've decided to read a surah from the Quran before taking the bus. I turn on the TV and land on a literary program. Ismail Kadaré is the guest. Impossible to turn it off. Always the same story. This tug-of-war within me between the Text and the texts. This morning, the writers have won out. I haven't read a line of the Quran. I watched the program. While waiting for the next bus, I leaf through a collection of poems by Nazim Hikmet. "Autobiography." In it, the author takes stock of his life. He wrote this text on September 11, 1961. I think again about the tug-of-war of texts. It is as if there were an invisible hand always guiding me, at the crucial moment, towards the texts I need. A strange phenomenon. As if the books are waiting for me there, on a shelf—some of them for centuries—confident in their truth. As if someone is guiding my encounters and tracing my path through books. And this *someone*, this great teacher, seems to be telling me: "Follow your path, be free!"

I remember the day when, after finishing *Journey to the End of the Night*, I wondered if Céline had been to Africa. Was he a medical doctor? Had he been to the United States and seen New York, the vertical city? I walked into a bookstore and came face-to-face with a book by his wife, Lucette Destouches—*My Life with Céline*. I read it right there. Of course, Céline had been in Africa, in Cameroun. He was a doctor. He traveled to the US for some kind of symposium and tried to find Molly. A fortuitous event? The result of destiny? Will? The eyes see because the spirit knows.

On the bus, I reach into the inside pocket of my jacket. I hesitate between *Notebook of a Return to the Native Land* and René Char's *Hypnos*. In the end I choose Captain Alexandre.[1] More abrupt. I cross the city with these words whose author says that they owe nothing to self-love, that they could just as well have been published by a fire of dry grass. That they were written under strain, in anger, fear, rivalry, furtive reflection, and the illusion of a future, friendship and love. Several kilometers of syllables down the road I get off the bus and run towards the driving school. It's raining. I miss the first six questions of the vehicle code. Once the class is finished, I go to have a coffee before heading for the lab. It's still raining. I think about her. Her presence haunts these places. Sweet wound. I walk across the alleyway fearlessly and remember two Algerian physicists who were living there, in the same building. One of them, from Oran, was kind, and the other, who had a tuft of white in his hair, had an uncompromising look and didn't talk much. I hurry up and look for that other face without its ugly masks, the pearl buried in the humus. Life goes on. The day has gone by quickly. I stayed late in the lab. I walk faster and hope to arrive on time.

Literary Time

Literary time obliterates chronological time. Despite the half-century that separates us, for the past few years Captain Alexandre has been my daily companion. A rich and silent dialogue. I look around me in this room and realize that my principal interlocutors are no longer here. Some of them withdrew from the phenomenal world centuries ago. They chose to communicate to the world in the most demanding way of all: a book. Our dialogue is all the more serene for it, stripped of the dross of life's daily froth and passing moods. Time has culled out empty words; only the pulse remains. Writing has this advantage over speech: it has had time to ripen. A book is the arrowhead of speech. It collects and shares the best of a life's vital impulses. It condenses the entire experience of the writer and of those who have persisted through him. It is an expansion, a deepening, and its elaboration has required the outflow of a vital energy, the consumption of an inner fire.

Captain Alexandre was born on the banks of the Sorgue river, between the Ventoux and Luberon regions, in a land of lavender, live oaks and vineyards. In 1941, while France was occupied by Nazi Germany, he decided to join the resistance. He explained his reasons to his friend Francis Curel in these terms: "After the disaster I didn't have the heart to return to Paris. I can only just persevere here, in a remote place I have chosen, but that I still find too close to the comings and goings of faces resigned to themselves and to things as they are. Of course it is still necessary to write poems, to trace with silent ink the rage and lamentations of our deadly state of mind, but that cannot be all. It would be absurdly insufficient."

These words attest to the act of commitment of a man who, faced with the sight of a *tortured victim's blood,* decides to leave behind the comfort and abstraction of books. In the face of horror, writing is certainly necessary, but literature remains absurdly insufficient. The pen dives deep into the self and collides with an inner demand; acts extend this necessity outwards.

Captain Alexandre decides to achieve the noblest of accords—to synchronize himself by leading a life that fuses acts and words. He writes to one of his friends: "I would urge caution, distance. Beware of complacent ants. Beware of those who say that they are hopeful because they are cooperating. It's not always easy to be intelligent and mute, contained and outraged. You know this better than anyone. Meanwhile, watch the water wheels of the Sorgue as they turn. Measure the lilting length of their foam. Calculate the dilapidated resistance of their boards. Confide quietly in the wild waters that we love. Then you will be prepared for the brutality that will be on brazen display. Is this the gateway to our dark end, you are asking? No. We are inside the unthinkable, but we have dazzling reference points."

What are these dazzling reference points? The sentries of poetry. "For every collapse of proofs, the poet responds with a salvo from the future."

The inhabitants of literary time who haunt this room share a concern for the construction of self, for autonomy, for independence and for freedom. They conceive their lives and live their thought.

To coincide with oneself. Meditate on that posture.

Everything Will Vanish

Everything will vanish. The cave paintings of Lascaux, the morning star, *Les Demoiselles d'Avignon*, people and their work. Life. The sun will die; the universe will be devoured by a black hole. Everything will vanish.

So why write, why create, why persist? Why plant trees that will outlive us, sculpt columns that will sing to us? Why pass on words, weave new melodies, build oblivion? Why?

Because art is a panegyric to the infinite. At the heart of beauty, time no longer exists. While our life is brief on a cosmic scale, contemplating beauty is its ultimate fulfillment. From one generation to another, artists pass on the ripe fruit of their quest. It is first immanent, then transcendent. Once again immanent, and once again transcendent.

Jihad

This book is a jihad. An inner war. A jihad to move outside myself, my race, my sex, my religion, my resolutions. A jihad to move towards myself. It is a desire for birth, and hence for death. To exist through my will for living, like the nascent Ptah. This book is a spillway of words. The ones I can no longer contain. The ones that are not smothered by my everyday concerns. The words that withstand the tram ride, the day's work, the vacuous prose, the daily ups and downs. Writing as a kind of overflowing, a kind of excess. The words that survive. The words that stand up to the circumscription of social time, to the confiscation of the present, to the squandering of time, to giving up, to fatigue, to abdication, to a slow death. These rescued words that lock arms to withstand the next squall. This book is a promise kept, a potentiality that finally comes to fruition. A post-term child, a late arrival. It is not Zulfiqar, Ali's double-pointed sword that cut off heads at the battle of Badr. Nor is it a confession, because there is nothing to confess.

It is a spiritual combat. Not the one carried out by anchorites or aesthetes. It does not aim to free soul from body or spirit from flesh. It is an attempt to "possess the truth in a soul and a body." This book is a Kalashnikov. The weapon of desire for freedom. The weapon that fires bursts at the social tank, at its tracks that flatten and level and oppress bodies and minds. This book is a jihad. A jihad for survival in a cynical, capitalist society. A jihad for rising above. A jihad against the tyranny of condition, and the group, and the couple. Jihad. Effort. A jihad against the perversion of the meaning of jihad. A jihad in the quest for peace. A jihad for knowledge becoming wisdom. A jihad for meaning, for *sapiens* against *demens*. A jihad against widespread brainwashing. A jihad for embracing the totality of the world. A jihad for living according to convictions. A jihad against toadyism and greed, a jihad against haste. A jihad for fullness, for emptiness, for awakening. A jihad against jihads. A jihad for fulfilling a multiple identity, for deploying all of one's wings, for flying, for overflowing, for approaching the sun and being consumed.

Bassai

I arrived at the place of the Path on time. The session hadn't begun yet. We came here to receive instruction, to revitalize ourselves, and to practice the art of the open hand. This art, practiced for centuries in secret, was *unveiled* by Shoto in Okinawa. It involves polishing the mind and the body to develop a pure awareness and face the world with complete clarity. The place of the path was a rare setting where one could still disengage from the turbulence of the outside world and work slowly and deeply. In an enclosed space one learned to be fully aware of oneself, free of compromise or deception. With honest introspection, the adversary is none other than oneself. The other, a partner who gives of his time so that you might climb the ladder of your being. Here one is both together and alone.

On the program for today's session: *Bassai*. The first movement consists in breaking through a circle in which one is enclosed. Break the fortifications. Breach the wall formed by the adversaries. Penetrate a fortress, crush its shell and become oneself. Move outside the circle and take possession of space and time. The next movements are parries of blows that come from the rear and the sides. The first counterattack does not occur until the eleventh movement. It shows respect for the adversary's life. He has been offered multiple chances to understand the futility of his actions. *Chudan Tsuki* in the solar plexus to put an end to his aggressive impulses. Breath, internal energy, Qi. The imaginary combat continues. Take root, connect to the ground, agglomerate one's mass with that of the Earth. Project the Qi with the help of the body by focusing the shock wave and the internal energy on a specific point: *Kime*. Projection of oneself into and through the adversary. Penetrate his mind before penetrating his body. Be one with him. Alternation of slow and rapid movements. Focus, rhythm, linked movements, hip thrusts. Work the forms slowly, then progressively increase the tempo and initiate *Kime*. Do not neglect the gesture. Do not let the spirit slip away, strengthen it with the moving body. Maintain self-presence in each act. Use the right gesture, the appropriate gesture. *Zanshin*, the spirit of gesture, of movement, the vigilant spirit, the spirit that abides without attachments. Take charge of the present action and remain attentive to what may occur.

The Climbers

Day after day I was scaling the works of Quignard from Verneuil, and Wilhelm from Saxony, and Milan from Prague, and Sédar from Djilor, and Mawlaana from Konya. They were unlocking doors in me, loosening folds buried in the deepest part of my being. Why is it that most writers do not relate the path of their awakening? Why do they not speak of those who shook them and roused them from sleep? Why do they give the impression that they were born of themselves? Why do they only evoke them after they are dead and buried? Are they afraid of meeting them? Are they afraid that mentioning those who preceded them will diminish their own brilliance?

The aim is to point out trails to the *climbers*, lighthouses to the *navigators*, oases to the *outlaws*. The aim here is a transmigration of force and light, a transfer of qualities and values from one human to another. The aim is to continue an ancient work, still unfinished (outside the paths of similarity).

Escape to Glory

As long as one lives there is the possibility of debasement, of becoming a shadow of oneself. Mishima killed himself at the height of his glory, in broad daylight, after completing his life's work. Checked out in the middle of the day. He'd had enough of the struggle. A fear of no longer being able to preserve the summits of ancient times, of losing the greatness he had achieved with such difficulty. Suicide as an honorable exit. Stig Dagerman killed himself because, he said, no oppressive force has a hold over silence. Suicide as the ultimate freedom, as an end to putting one's life on the chopping block of time. Achilles preferred the brief but glorious life of a warrior to the long but anonymous life of a peasant. To move towards a certain death, to leave behind the best of oneself, to be sublimated. The one who is remembered never dies.

Periods of war are conducive to this kind of fervor. Some ordinary men go to war secretly hoping for a glorious death on the field of honor and thereby surviving in the memory of their peers and becoming a part of their family's legend. Disguised suicide. The quest for glory. Herostratus, in his quest for glory, burned down the temple of Artemis. His contemporaries condemned his name to silence—no one was allowed to utter it aloud. But the future proved him right, and his name did not sink into oblivion. In Paestum, a man leapt past the columns of Hercules into the ocean of death. Rather than a legacy, he chose to leave behind a tale of death. This suicide was immortalized in a fresco: the Tomb of the Diver. The unknown man achieved immortality in this way. These suicides are escapes. Greatness consists in accepting every aspect of one's humanity—the *adret* and the *ubac*. Accepting reality, as it is. To experience the peak of one's existence but also to endure one's decline and go on living despite it all. Wilhelm from Saxony was a radical writer. Early on he suffered from migraines, contemplated suicide on several occasions, but resisted. On January 1, 1882, in Genoa, he wrote: "I still live, I still think: I still have to live, for I still have to think." He understood that the condition for extreme joy was extreme pain. He endured his physical pain and his solitude, as well as the incomprehension and rejection of his contemporaries. He held out *patiently, severely, coldly, without submitting, but also without hope*. He reconciled himself to every aspect of his humanity, did what he had to do, and gave mankind one of the most courageous, lucid and liberating works that has ever existed. He descended into madness toward the end of his life, in Turin, upon seeing a horse being abused by a coachman. He died ten days after the first Assumption Day of a twentieth century that would consecrate his glory.

Esther Mujawayo

Esther Mujawayo, a Rwandan psychotherapist and survivor of the genocide, lives in Germany with her new husband. Her fifteen-year-old daughter asks her: "Was Primo Levi Italian?" "Yes!" she replies. There is no rivalry of suffering here. These Tutsi survivors read Primo Levi and talk about him to their children. Their experiences are similar; the racial and socio-economic contingencies are irrelevant. People find themselves naked in their condition and in the universal mystery of its cruelty. Boubacar Boris Diop, Abdourahman Waberi, Véronique Tadjo, and Jean Hatzfeld have written indispensable works on the genocide of the Tutsi of Rwanda. Naming the unnamable. Thinking the unthinkable. Bearing witness to the dark zone of our humanity—remembering it, facing it, trying to understand it to keep it distant. Because for now, that's what is at stake—keeping evil at a distance. The genocide of the Tutsi of Rwanda: a collective defeat of humanity. For three months, some men massacred others with machetes and axes. A million people died while the whole world watched. Those who were capable of acting did nothing. They stood up belatedly, lazily, casually—their intentions vague—and made a pretense of dressing wounds. The UN withdrew its troops and personnel and left behind observers *to observe* Africans massacring other Africans. Murder through language had begun before the genocide. A desensitization and dehumanization through words. These human beings were degraded to the status of cockroaches to be exterminated. Prior to the infliction of bodily harm, spoken words always pave the way. To debase humanity, reduce it, before committing the crime. Speech that is dehumanizing, anathematizing, racist, fascist, disrespectful and insulting is the prelude to all barbarism. It is certain that one day other men will come along with words to deny the genocide of the Tutsi of Rwanda, minimize its infamy and clear the names of those responsible for it. That is why *Murambi: The Book of Bones, Harvest of Skulls, Machete Season*, and *The Shadow of Imana* are indispensable books.

Thanks to You

Thanks to you, Milan, it all starts with a phrase in *The Unbearable Lightness*… "mindless monogamy," then *Immortal, Testaments Betrayed,* and all your work until your sulking in *Ignorance,* which I didn't care for but I ended up raising the *curtain* on. Thanks to you, Hermann, it all began with *Siddhartha, Narcissus and Goldmund,* and then came *Demian, The Glass Bead Game* and all your work, and the meaning it passed on to me. Sometimes I dream about Joseph K and Castalia, and the *vicus lusorum*. Thank you for helping me to undertake the *Journey to the East.* Thanks to you, Jean-Paul, it began with *The Words,* then *Dirty Hands, The Respectful Prostitute,* then all your work. Thank you for teaching me that man creates himself, that he is not a prisoner of his origins and determinations. My thanks to you, Pascal, it all began with *The Roving Shadows,* existing in the blind spot, *in angulo,* then *Sex and Terror, La leçon de musique, A Terrace in Rome, The Last Kingdom,* and all your work that speaks to inner freedom. I sensed an affection

21

for Jansenism in it, and I drew strength and courage from it. Thank you, the silent one from Harar. Thank you, Philippe, it began with *Passion fixe,* then *Eloge de l'infini* and culminated with *Une vie divine.* Thank you, René Char. Thank you, Rumi, for having burned me. Thank you, Gibran, for your profound wisdom. Thank you, Dante, the winged man. Thank you, Friedrich. Thank you, Rilke, for your *Letters to a Young Poet,* which taught me to love questions, and that art must occupy a true place in the life of the artist, that art is awakening and spiritual rebirth. Your letters taught me to accept and endure pain and suffering, the joy and loneliness of the creator, and to welcome the newness that is created in me, to nourish the growth of my inner universe, to become a world. Thank you, Uncle Nesta. Thank you, Senghor. Thank you, Césaire. Thank you, Pablo, for your life and for rewarding my gaze with light and color. Thanks to you, the Seer of Le Creusot, imprisoned in the cradle of light that your pen reflects. Thank you, Jacques Lacarrière, for your *Sourates* and their radicalism. Thanks to my friends. Thanks to Jean-Paul D., my teacher and companion on the path. My enemies have not defeated me.

Endurance

Jihad. Intense effort. Endure your weaknesses, wipe them away one by one. Endure fatigue, the daily trials, the steep passes. Endure the demands on yourself at every moment. Endure the effort. Strive for the heights. Endure the heights. Endure speech. Endure words. Endure silence. Endure all these things until the feeling of self-importance is extinguished. And, on that day, there is nothing more to endure, because the self that endured is dead.

The peaceful walk betrays the long walk. The one that demands patience, endurance and proportionate pace. A gait reveals a lot about the inner mechanics of the walker. Determination or resignation, defeat or victory. Self-mastery, complacency, a sense of security. Suppleness, agility, the cat's gait, the ambling gait of an elephant, the heavy, low-slung gait of a hen, the cackling cock walk. Walking broadens horizons.

Rain reveals people's character—when they are taken by surprise by something incongruous. The sudden exposure causes some part of conventional attitudes to loosen a bit. A dash for shelter, an accelerated step, acceptance of things as they are, foresight—everyone reveals their relationship with personal comfort. Women smile more readily, caught off guard in a state of slight intimacy that scarcely embarrasses them, like when they stumble, nearly fall and you catch them. Unmasked by sudden incongruities.

Fana, the Annihilation of Self

The attempt to extinguish the self through spirituality is always a persistence of the ego. It is the self that endures in its desire to be, to attain, in its striving toward fulfilment.

*

The self wants to be modest. The ambition for humility is not vulgar, but it is no less real.

*

The immodesty of conspicuously wearing the cloak of humility.

*

Silence, an extreme form of freedom.

*

Dahij

To annihilate oneself is to find one's place in the universal harmony of things. It is to beat at the same rhythm as the pulse of the universe. A heartbeat requires no effort; it labors at rest.

*

To annihilate oneself is to be here, naturally. Here, now, deeply, intensely, permanently, absolutely.

Shift in Perspective

Fadel took a seat on the tram facing backwards. He decided not to read, to free up his head and to let his mind wander. The weather was gray and cold. Suddenly, on the George V bridge, above the Loire, there was a burst of light. White, iridescent. The rays of the sun like laser beams radiated through his whole being, burned away his tumors of melancholy and dismay. He had always thought of such sudden bursts of light that changed his mood as a sign that nothing was permanent. He had devised a maxim from this observation: "States of mind pass, wait." It took less than a minute to cross the Loire. Every morning, he took care to contemplate the river, even if for only an instant. The first day, he saw nothing. Then, little by little, he noticed its different colors, its rising levels, its low water mark, the small islets that appeared and disappeared, the pathways along its banks, the violence of the walls that contained it, its torpor on rainy days, its fickle power, its impermanence. Gray, dark, greenish, languid, impetuous. Tibetan monks spend days at a time making mandalas with grains of colored sand, destroying them as soon as they are completed to signify the transitory nature of material life. Day after day crossing the Loire had become a moment of contemplation, an ersatz infinity. His gaze also needed to be educated. A daily contemplation of the fifth figure in the *Demoiselles d'Avignon* on the illuminated side of the wall. Something distinctive in her look, the darker face, more striated, more masked, more troubling, and that black left eye. A few moments every day for contemplating a piece of the universe. Artwork displayed in open air. The Loire, still gray, greenish, languid, calm, raging, permanent, impermanent.

Fadel got off the tram, crossed the Martroi square in the rain and headed for the Crédit Lyonnais ATM. He printed the balance on his account and slipped the paper into his pocket. Along the way he glanced at it, mentally calculated the three hundred euros of overdraft allowed and realized that he wouldn't have enough. That dampened his enthusiasm a bit. He walked into the Fnac bookstore, rethinking his needs. He had planned to buy some blank discs, an ink cartridge, a few books and maybe a record, if he could find something worth his time. There was a buzz of activity in the store and he wondered why. Ah! It was the eve of the Toussaint holiday weekend. He headed over to the "New Titles" section. It was the season of literary prizes and the Goncourt and the Femina had just been awarded. He picked up Alice Ferney's *Dans la guerre*, read the summary on the back of the book and leafed through the first pages. He really didn't like the paper Actes Sud used to print its novels, a kind of brownish paper and a typeface that looked like oversized writing for adolescents. The story took place during the First World War. Some of its elements—a call for general mobilization, a few of the characters and especially a dog with human feelings—were enough to discourage him. Despite being the favorite, Alice Ferney had just failed to win the Goncourt. She came in third place, behind Beigbeder and Amette. She had also just barely missed out on the Femina a few years back. Although he had some misgivings, he decided to have a look at Beigbeder's *Windows on the World.* He had read his previous novel, *99 Francs*, and had found the idea of a critique of the advertising world timely, but the writing left him cold. These writers appearing on TV all the time puzzled him. He preferred those who, opting for the truth and shadows of the novel, rarely showed up on television screens. The first pages of *Windows on the World* were well written. But his misgivings won out in the end, and he decided not to buy it. The author had built up an image of himself as a lighthearted dandy with a penchant for self-mockery, which had made him into a congenial figure in the eyes of the public. But then we don't ask writers to be congenial. Fadel opened Jacques-Pierre Amette's *Brecht's Mistress*, which had won the Goncourt, and felt a little sheepish for choosing the same book as everyone else. The first few pages flowed nicely. It was the same funneling technique that he found in a lot of authors. Describe a general situation, a place, and then gradually introduce the characters. Yet he had the feeling that this was a standardized way of writing, clean and smooth. The mark of great writers was in the singularity of their style. They had a *language*. He was interested in Brecht's personal history, and he had read *A Short Organum* , and he had never heard of Jacques-Pierre Amette. So, he decided to buy the book. *Libération*, the novel by Ablaye Diop, was in a section behind the one with the best sellers, where Beigbeder, Amette, and Alice Ferney were on prominent display. On the back cover of the book was a posed-looking photo of Diop smiling with a faraway look in his eyes. Fadel had already read the book with attention and curiosity. In it, Ablaye Diop had explored the inner path of deconditioning, solitude and self-mastery. It was a good book. The author had traced his transformations, and his language had a marked pungency. Yet Fadel was critical of the occasional lack of complexity, a few overly idealized portraits, some shortcuts at times, a few subtle compromises with the zeitgeist, and especially some artfully novelized biographical details. Therein lies all the art and ambiguity of the novel. You couldn't criticize a novel simply for being one. Most people consider the seemingly autobiographical stories related in a novel to be true. They identify the narrator with the author. What often interests the voyeur-reader these days are details of the author's private life *betrayed* by the act of writing. When Ablaye Diop relates in a fictionalized manner his first encounter with literature thanks to a couple of French aid workers who introduced him to Alexandre Dumas, Hugo, Chateaubriand and many others, Fadel knew that this detail, inspired from his personal history, was not altogether accurate.

He and Diop were living together at the time and Diop was keen on the kind of comics called *aventures* in Dakar, which tell the tales of the trials and tribulations of Zembla or Blek the rock or Tex Willer the Texan sheriff. He recalled the efforts he had made to get Ablaye to read his first novel—and there were no French aid workers in sight. He could have countered with "But it's a novelistic truth!" But Ablaye Diop was clearly aware that Western readers were fond of the kind of story in which a little African boy is saved from the obscurantism and oppression of his society by the wisdom of their literature and its heralds. Especially when during some of his television interviews he was asked: "Is it true that your two *coopérant* friends were amazing people who made a big difference in your life?" he would nod in agreement, without elaborating further. It was just part of the construction of the author's persona. And it was clearly a more romantic account—to be freed from a dismal fate by the force of knowledge and words, with the help of a couple of *coopérants*, was a version that would delight Western readers and stroke their narcissism as emissaries of universal enlightenment.

Fadel walked out of the bookstore and ran to catch the bus, but the driver (who had noticed him) didn't wait. He had to brave the bitter cold of this unusual autumn. He paused for a moment and looked around him at the streets teeming with people, the faces passing by, the striated walls, the stones marked by time. He walked to the bus shelter and observed its confined space. He took in the fresh air and the cold. On the bus, he chose a seat facing backwards. He liked this position because it gave him the feeling that the city was swallowing him. There was no more horizon—everything was happening behind him, and the buildings and streets came into view once he was already submerged in them. Fadel meditated on the profusion of literary works on offer. This country, more than any other, had to be the one where the figure of the writer lit up people's fantasies. Even French presidents were jealous of their status. When Mitterrand visited René Char at Les Busclats, he wanted to sit in the poet's armchair.

But alas, this overabundance of books was no guarantee of quality. The market was flooded. You could occasionally come across some lovely works whose words were true and original. But surrounding these rare fruit trees was a forest of lurid offerings—books in which authors unpacked their petty grievances, books that accommodated the social demand for exoticism, books that complacently mirrored the spirit of the times and reinforced its platitudes.

Where were the others, Fadel wondered, the ones that attempted to move closer to some truth? Lost in the crowd. Overabundance was the new form of censorship. Those rare authors who were honest and shunned the media circus were likely to see their works float by unnoticed. The most fortunate among them would be displayed for a few days in a bookstore and then back they'd go to the publisher and the pulp pile for lack of demand. These were the implacable rules of the market. Stock management, just-in-time production, minimization of costs, maximization of profits. Books that didn't generate a buzz within the first few days of release were not kept on the shelves. In this environment, the value of a work was determined by its sales numbers. And to increase sales, you had to activate the networks of pen-pushers and professionals of enthusiastic and obliging reviews. You make the rounds of all the outlets of publicity and self-promotion. In short, you had to be seen on all the TV interview shows and reviewed in all the important media. The publishers' press officers ranked the different programs by the number of book sales they generated. They knew that an appearance on a given show during a prime-time hour was equal to ten thousand copies flying off the shelves the next day. Book sellers were informed a month in advance so that they could order sufficient stock. The system for influencing consumer tastes was finely tuned. For vainglorious authors, the ones in whom the echoes of Narcissus muted the demands of inner truth, there began the endless wandering in the vicious circles of compromise and self-denial. Merchants of cultural products encouraged them to play their part in the symphony of the times and embrace their assigned role and place. Blurt out a few secrets on a talk show, highlight two or three neuroses —in short, a little prostitution—and you're done. In this field of ruin, some authors had given up on interacting with their contemporaries. They had left the playground and carried on with their work in secret. They had become the counterpoint of their times. In a world where nobody was listening to anyone anymore, amid all the noise and commotion, they no longer raised their voices. The most radical of them had even given up writing altogether. Their work became simply the embodiment of their thought. They no longer even distilled *their thoughts for themselves.* Who knows, an unscrupulous relative could publish them postmortem, after adding a few conformist touchups and rewordings. In the face of widespread exhibitionism: modesty. In the face of over-communication: secrecy. Set themselves in opposition to the world. Black holes retaining a light that could not be diffused, a refusal of false understandings and gossip. Other seekers of light gathered in small circles to develop an ethics of resistance. They thought that the resistance had to build its networks, make themselves known, encourage others to join them, focus on the long term, *to enlarge, until it becomes light, which will always be fleeting, the glimmer during which we're shaken, we begin to act, and we persist.*

When he got home, Fadel turned on his computer and opened the file labeled "Jihad." He started a new chapter, which he entitled "Change of Perspective."

During the act of writing, forget the world. Drive the pen into the deepest part of yourself. Take note of whatever rises to the surface, without taboos or moral judgement or censorship. Construct your words in complete freedom. Pay no attention to the times, don't think about the advice of those close to you or your contemporaries. A book is one of the rare places where you can speak without lying, without conforming to the multiple variations of a predetermined discourse, without giving in to ideological presuppositions and evaluations. Free up the words, renew them, deflate the clichés.

Whoever consciously constructs his work to please the greatest number of readers by indulging popular expectations prostitutes himself. He perverts an act of supreme freedom. All writers are intimately aware of the moment when they bargain with their inner truth, the moment when they resort to tricks, when they make themselves more beautiful or less attractive than they are. The act of writing is an act of self-deconstruction. You let down your hair and bid farewell to the social lie and its false truths. Suspending moral judgement is the morality of the novel, says Milan from Prague. Reality must be revealed such as it is, not as it should be. In the space of writing, marginality is not a posture, which by creating strangeness creates something rare, and hence something interesting. It is inherent. To write is to be alone.

Singhiam

Singhiam and Bouba were friends during their adolescence. They had both been students at Sacré-Coeur school and had completed their baccalaureate degrees there. After graduation, their paths diverged. Bouba came to France to study math at the Jussieu campus of the Sorbonne. One day, they arranged to meet in the 14th arrondissement, at the Saint-Jacques student residence. It had been seven years since they had last seen each other. The neighborhood seemed calm and affluent. Wide avenues, 19th-century architecture, Hausmannian buildings, a few tobacco shops on the street corners. It was far removed from the teeming cosmopolitanism of some of the neighborhoods in the 18th arrondissement. Not a single Greek sandwich shop or noisy bar in sight. The air seemed heavy with a kind of protestant austerity. Bouba welcomed his friend into a university dorm room as austere as the ambient air. There was a table, a bed, a closet, a sink, a treatise on algebra and probability theory, and a few physics and atomistic chemistry books on the table.

Beside the bed was the holy Quran and a collection of hadiths by Boukari and Muslim. Bouba was clearly happy to see his friend. And yet there was something reserved about his delight, and this reserve dampened his enthusiastic nature a bit.

"How's it going, boy?" Singhiam asked. "You haven't changed much, except for the beard. Looking for a more manly face?"

"*Alhamdullillah*, I'm getting by," he replied calmly. "But you've changed—you look like a movie star."

"Stop it—me, a movie star?"

"I hear you've become an artist. Have you given up on being president or is it just a phase?"

"That was just a childhood fantasy. I'm still interested in politics, of course, but I can't stand politicians. I can't see how you can get into politics these days without being corrupt."

Bouba's only response was a wry smile. It was the time of day for the *tisbaar* prayer.[2] Bouba said to his friend: "Let's pray! Are you keeping up with your prayers?"

"Of course!"

"You sure? You're an artist now," he said, with a look that was part mocking, part skeptical.

"And so—artists don't pray?"

"You know, sometimes they think they're God—it seems they *create*. And they often have some strange moral standards, everyone knows that."

Singhiam smiled and shook his head wearily. They performed their ablutions and prayed. He wanted to give Bouba the honor of leading the prayer, but he refused. Singhiam was married and he wasn't. So, it was up to Singhiam to serve as imam. In the Muslim tradition, given equal levels of erudition, it is the married man who leads the prayer. He is assumed to be more chaste or at least to have more settled morals. They spent the whole afternoon together, dug up some old memories, spoke of their lives as expatriates, or exiles, or immigrants, or migrants—they no longer knew which term to use. Singhiam avoided subjects that might cast a shadow over this lovely reunion. His friend had become deeply religious. He sensed that he was somewhat intolerant and a little overly conscious of his virtue, as though this was a recent discovery. He made hasty judgments on a lot of subjects, and his ideas weren't open to discussion. Bouba reminded him of their talks when they were students at Sacré-Coeur. He alluded to several things and seemed to be saying: "I'm no fool, you know. Everything you're doing today is part of a carefully laid out plan. You are ambitious! You want to succeed in this world. Even your refusal to apply for French citizenship isn't because of pride or integrity. It's because you have political ambitions and you're afraid that French nationality might thwart them." "Don't worry," he said with a laugh, "our president, Abjoulaye Wade, has French nationality and a French wife as well." All these innuendos had bothered him. What did Bouba know about him to speak like this? In fact, he no longer knew him. Moreover, had he ever really known him? No, he hadn't foreseen or planned anything. Singhiam had come to understand that life was filled with a lot more imagination than dreams or plans. Everything that had happened to him over these past years was completely unexpected—ups and downs, chance encounters, revelations. He hadn't taken French nationality for the simple reason that to do so would mean for him to belong to a community, to be prepared if necessary to defend it against its enemies, but also against its own demons. It would mean sharing its values, but especially, feeling accepted. Everyone who knew that his wife was French naturally thought that he too had become French through marriage, as though it were a given. Some didn't even bother asking him the question. There was a tacit complicity among certain immigrants on this point. What's it to you? We all know that we marry them for that. The French thought the same thing. No, he had married his wife because of a simple desire to live with her and start a family, the classic reason. Furthermore, he was determined to complete his projects while maintaining his nationality of origin. Yes, French nationality would allow him to travel, but this was not the key to paradise and didn't make him a better or happier person. And above all, if you were someone with his lovely anthracite color, no one mistook you for a Frenchman. For now, in the collective imagination, the word French corresponded to an individual with white skin, and neither Zidane nor Thuram could do much to change that. One of his friends who was born here, a *natural-born* citizen, was regularly asked for his residence permit in various administrations and had trouble renting an apartment or getting job interviews despite a more than respectable university education. On the hundreds of CVs that he would send out, there was always, alas, his lovely photo and his foreign-sounding surname. There were Frenchmen and then there were *natural-born,* and it wasn't the same thing. It's true! Whenever there was another global upheaval and everyone was called on to state which camp they were in, the *natural-born* were always suspected of disloyalty to the national community. Might they not be the fifth column of the invaders? The enemy's trojan horse? French diplomats did not provide the same level of support to the *natural-born* who encountered problems in faraway lands. In city halls, he had very often heard the whispered suspicions of civil registrars when officiating mixed marriages. And then there was the humiliating interview you were subjected to, when you would be asked, in passing, why you wanted to be French and if you disliked your country of origin. As though by giving you this piece of paper—which, of course, you had to deserve—they were providing you access to a higher level of humanity. To get there, you not only had to prove your love for *la douce France* but also to provide evidence that you were not infected with an epizootic disease—that you were suitable to join the herd that had reserved the rights to the greenest pastures on the planet. It's true! But this was only a piece of paper, we were all human, and one's nationality was supposed to be a minor detail. Through the most miraculous piece of good fortune, everyone was born on some part of the planet. No special merit in that. But this mania for incessantly knocking on the door even though the hosts have made it clear that you are not welcome! And then there were certain members of the Global

South elite who brandished their hard-earned French nationality like a promotion, proud of having been finally accepted, finally anointed and dubbed!

After several years spent in this land, Singhiam now had his bearings. He had re-created himself and had pieced together new loyalties. Little by little, he started to feel more connected to the country. Cities, places, streets now brought back moments of his personal history. He had, despite its monsters, begun to love some of its faces, but he still couldn't bring himself to acquire the nationality, as everyone advised him to do. Even if it was only to keep seeing his children if one day things didn't work out with his wife, because they would tell him: "Everyone knows that judges automatically grant custody of the children to the mothers, and especially when the father is African!" He was counseled to acquire it so that he could travel and get health care and because: "You never know what might happen in Africa—you don't want to be stuck if things get bad. Cover your back." Common sense advice or the age-old fear of becoming? Could you really protect yourself from all of life's pitfalls? Others proposed a realist, dispassionate argument: "They prevent us from traveling on this planet, which is a legitimate right of every human being; they prevent us from beginning, from finding our fulfillment. You've got nothing to prove! Just take it, the piece of paper, it's not going to change you. Forget about it and carry on with your life, it's just one more tool to get ahead and take care of your family. You're just granting yourself something normal, the freedom of movement!"

And yet he had the feeling that doing this would put the seal on a kind of *de-solidarity* with his people. Afterwards, they would no longer share the same destiny. He would no longer have to stand in long lines in front of embassies, furnish a mountain of documents and at times humiliate himself to obtain a hypothetical visa. If he no longer had to experience these iniquities, he would be less inclined to work to make them go away. He'd find himself in the camp of the well-to-do; he'd have a passport and be able to leave whenever things went badly—but not them. He had always known that he wouldn't hesitate to return to his native land if one day they started to refuse him the possibility of remaining here with his dignity intact. And moreover, he hadn't yet decided where he was going to live in the coming years. He would not join any protests, or hunger strikes like the undocumented workers in Saint-Bernard, whose struggle for recognition seemed legitimate to him. But it troubled him how some people clung to this corner of the planet. A little dignity, dammit! He had never seen himself in the miserabilism and pessimism that made Africa out to be a monolithic bloc and the breeding ground for all the world's woes. It wasn't about denying the very real difficulties that these courageous and noble people encountered in their efforts to over-come. But there was something falsely reassuring in portraying others in this way, in only seeing them through their wounds. The other often defines us through antinomy. The blacker he is, the better our whiteness appears to us. His miseries bring to light our good fortune, which out of long habit we can no longer see. What better antidepressant is there? A little dose of blues music and then a news report on Liberia reminds you of the peace and security and comfort you enjoy, along with the quality and the vast organizational capabilities of your society, to which you have of course contributed! And bingo, you can toss your box of Prozac overboard and at the same time contribute to reducing the deficit of the national health insurance. These news reports out of Africa have all kinds of beneficial effects! And if you are African, don't even think about trying to clarify or qualify these *truths*. Obviously, you are not objective, and you don't want to face up to the reality—which by the way is another explanation of why this continent is still in such a sorry state. Just look at the people who would rather die on the paths of illegal immigration than live back there! Look at the wars and the famines! And you're telling us that things are OK? One Stephen Smith, for his work in cataloguing a series of African catastrophes, embellished with alarming statistics and crowned with a shocking title, *Négrologie,* achieved great success and received literary prizes. Complexity is not simple, but that is our work! Stirring up fantasies and fears is, as everyone knows, easy, and it pays. Some African writers who have dealt with the ills of this continent fell into a trap—that of no longer being able to evoke the other side of the coin: Life. The inevitable retort was: "But it is you yourself who talk about it in your book: child soldiers, chronic wars, excision and on and on. It is true that this continent is appalling!" Others had made the *simpler* choice of serving up a simplistic, superficial discourse that went down well in this region, thereby demonstrating their qualities of objectivity, which the master could appreciate with a chuckle. At last, some unbiased Africans! Free! Who say things as they are, freed from their burdensome traditions! Attention, dear reader, we're not settling any scores! We are only doing our job, which is to disentangle truths from falsehoods and dismantle some intellectual traps. Once again, the goal is to embrace complexity by attempting to grasp truths as closely as possible—even closer!

Singhiam had traveled on the continent and had come to understand that there were multiple *Africas*, that some parts of this continent were more culturally different from each other than France and Senegal are. He had been all over in his country, lived in cities and rural areas, spent time with people from all walks of life. Naturally, some areas were better off than others, but even in the poorest places in his country people were not starving and had normal lives. They were poor perhaps, according to macroeconomic indicators, but they were not impoverished. Moreover, these indicators didn't mean much when you were living there. People lived, loved, strived, coped with daily ups and downs, had hopes and successes and failures, raised their children and had fulfilling lives. Viewed in this way, everything had meaning and value and proportion. Wealth and poverty were relative concepts. Rich in what way? Poor in what way? Rich relative to whom and to what? Developed how? Underdeveloped in what way? In humanity? In percentage points of GDP? In life experiences? In wisdom? In awakenings?

Staying in France was not an end in itself. He wasn't prepared to do so at any price. He could easily have taken on a different nationality—Venezuelan, Chinese, Swedish, Malian—just to show that, having lived among them, he now felt himself fraternally one of them. But alas, fraternity is not decreed unilaterally—both sides must want it. If at least his hosts had invited him with respect and love to the table of fraternity, he might well consider their offer. But for the moment, this was not the case. Hence there was no question of adopting this nationality. A little dignity, dammit! No, he wasn't ambitious, in any event he didn't have the kind of ambition described by the chattering masters—succeed socially, acquire power, etc. No. He wanted to elevate his soul, to sharpen his sensibility, understand existence, fathom its complexity. He wanted to construct his humanity, to live and be free. To settle down where he would be of use. That was his ambition, and it had been for some time. And then, we don't live on bread and water alone! Right, Jalal ad-Din?

Singhiam was annoyed with himself for replying "Of course!" when Bouba asked him if he had said his morning prayer. After all, the prayers were addressed to God. He didn't need to justify himself to anyone. He was free and responsible and could choose to do them or not—without reporting back to anyone. He had often encountered this questioning of his religious practice in Senegal. Have you done your prayers? Are you keeping the fast? In some families, the father forces the whole family to fulfill this ritual obligation. It is his duty to educate his family in Islam and hence no one can evade it.

He recalled one time when he arrived at the home of some friends at the time of the afternoon prayer. The father stood up ceremoniously and invited everyone present to observe this high holy obligation. Singhiam had not performed his morning prayers. Consequently, he would have had to get caught up before performing the present prayer (in accordance with doctrine), excuse himself, say that he was behind on his prayers, and accept incurring the suspicious gaze of the master of the house, being classified in the category of *disreputable friends*, and a sermon on the salat and the horrors of hell for those who neglect it. It was a lot to take on. Sometimes it was even more complicated. If he was in a state of great impurity, normal ablutions were not enough to purify him, and so the *janaba,* the great purifying bath, was called for. There were two ways to find oneself in a state of great impurity—either you were having your menstrual period, or you had recently had sexual intercourse. Since the first contingency didn't concern him, his intimacy would thus be exposed. Singhiam preferred in that case to get down on the mat. He assumed his most pious air, performed the prayer with everyone else, knowing deep down that it was simply gymnastics: bending over, extension, genuflection. At least it helped him to stay flexible.

With old Abdoulaye, this question was tinged with gentleness, and he would speak to his heart, without judgment. He would remind him of the ill effects of negligence. He would tell him to remember God, and to draw strength and comfort from this remembrance. He would tell him that we had to focus on the essential things, remember that we were only passersby on this earth, that we were responsible for the direction of the world and that we were accountable to it. The time granted to us was measured. What have we done with it? He would tell him that the prayer was a pause in daily activities. It allowed us to stand back, to focus, to be conscious of ourselves and to question the meaning of our acts, and our goals and purposes. Even when we had difficulty concentrating, besieged with everyday thoughts, prayer allowed us to glimpse the extent to which we were caught up in worldly affairs. Prayer was effort and fidelity. Fidelity to the remembrance of God in joy as in pain. It helped to reform one's being.

Unfortunately, for most people—uncles, cousins, the marabout passing through town, El Hadj Soandso, Sheikh Whatshisname—prayer sounded like a terrible call to order, a formal demand, an inquisition, a break-in to his consciousness and his intimacy. In a Muslim society, this was a legitimate question. A Muslim had the obligation to call his fellow man back to the path of righteous behavior and the observance of cultural practices. Mutual surveillance, social control. This kind of questioning was normal, could come from just about anyone, and was immune to the retort: "What the hell difference does it make to you if I pray or not? Are you God?" From the moment you are a Muslim, you have already adhered to the principles of Islam, and consequently you could be questioned about these principles; the obligations of Islam were right there, clear and precise. Others could legitimately confront you with them,

48

unless you were no longer part of the community. Singhiam had observed that most people who took the liberty of expressing this call to order did not do so out of a concern for offering guidance; otherwise, they would have gone about it more carefully and tactfully. They would have shown compassion, understanding and love prior to their reminder of the principle and the judgment. They would have tried to speak to their interlocutor's heart. Instead, they did it primarily because uttering this reminder, in addition to allowing themselves to become intoxicated with the awareness of their virtue and enhancing their self-image as a pious, respected Muslim—significant attributes in a Muslim society—also gave them power over you. They could expropriate the transcendence of which they claimed to be the heralds, for their own benefit. They could anoint themselves as spiritual advisors and meddle in matters that were none of their business. They could interrogate you, scrutinize you, judge you without knowing you, and all of that in the name of God. That was the essential part of the perfidy. *Apparently*, you could not object to such an attitude without objecting to divine directives. Saying "I don't pray" was the equivalent of "I don't respect divine injunctions." Which is unthinkable for a Muslim. And yet the prophet Mohammed, the perfect example of a Muslim, had said to his companions who were instructed to preach the good word: "Speak to them in the best of ways." In the Quran, several verses are addressed to the prophet in this way: "Warn because you are only a warner," and again: "There shall be no compulsion in [acceptance of] the

religion. The right course has become clear from the wrong."
These inquisitors must have been unaware of such verses. By
justifying himself to his friend, he had allowed him to intrude
into his privacy, to hold him accountable, to judge him. He had
granted his friend power over him. The question often came
out of the blue, caught you by surprise and, without thinking,
you would give in to self-justification—which allowed the
other person to take root in your consciousness and soon erect
a throne there. And the *burglars* of consciousness knew this.

In France, where Muslims were in the minority and not
generally welcomed, the question was stated in a different way.
You were asked whether you were a practicing Muslim. Which
meant: are you a "soft" Muslim, capable of being assimilated
into our culture? Do you drink wine, eat pork? Are you open
and moderate? Or are you orthodox, fundamentalist, and hence
not very open-minded, potentially dangerous and possibly a
terrorist? There were only two alternatives. A normal Muslim
became open or moderate. The adjective "moderate" served to
soften the presumed intrinsically violent charge of the noun
"Muslim." It served to clip the claws of the Islamic beast. Ever
since the Church, despite the glorious chapters of a history that
nurtured culture and beauty, had become guilty of the Inquisition and lost ground, and since spiritual matters occupied less
space in modern life, piety and scrupulous religious practice had
become suspect. The era of frenzied entertainment, of moral
laxity, and of a hedonism unworthy of its forebears, ignored any
notion of commitment, responsibility or demanding standards.

July 26, 2003

My initial idea was to drop by a bookstore and pick up a few books for the family. Sun Tzu for my father, Amin Maalouf for my mother and Rilke for my brother. As I rounded a corner, the *I Ching* was sitting there waiting for me. It practically summoned me to come looking for it. It had already been a few weeks since I began thinking about it, but I figured that such an old man would be difficult to find, especially in these times so rife with the cult of youth, so I had abandoned the idea of looking for it.

An altercation between the security guards and a suspected thief. While escorting him to a room in the back of the store they shoved him and shouted at him, roughed him up. Violence. Physical assault and humiliation before they even confirmed their suspicions. What were they really after, these guards?

I headed for the philosophy section and picked up *The Gay Science*, which I'd decided to pay a visit to after returning from *Zarathustra*. I furtively looked around for *Ecce Homo*, but nothing. I decided to take the *Inferno* with me to Dakar to reread, along with *The Gay Science*, the *I Ching* and Thucydides. I hoped that a month would be enough to get through them all.

Logbook

Nietzsche can wait until Mbao. First off, the road to Rufisque. Four narrow lanes lined with businesses in the industrial zone. Traffic jams, dangerous passing, *rapid buses.* At the rear of each vehicle, an aphorism to ward off bad luck. Suffocating heat, exhaust fumes, horns honking, snail's pace. Mopeds weaving in and out. To make forward progress you've got to have a rebellious spirit. Yield nothing. It's the jungle. Drivers pass on the right and the left, wander off the pavement, create new lanes. Headlights flashing, lane cutting, last-second swerves. Yet somehow all this chaos is under control, organized. No collisions today, no accidents. From this chaos an order is born.

Rufisque. Some call it Rio Fresco. A flood of memories. The Gabard square, the sea, the waves, the big limestone rocks. An unforgettable concert by Super Diamono at the Abdoulaye-Sadji lycée. The sewers. Walid the Lebanese had a fabric store in the center of town. The lingering spirit of Ousmane Socé Diop, the smell of bread at the Bargny garage. The Omar Samb stationary store, where I bought Cheikh Anta Diop's *Nations nègres et culture*. The police and the dread. Abasse Ndione's *Life in a Spiral. Keuri Kaw.* Primary school at the Immaculate Conception. Mr. Texeira. The huge clouds of smoke billowing from the Sococim plant. The Boye brothers' guitar duo. The public gardens. A mad philosopher who smeared the walls with proverbs. The Saltigués basketball team. The power plant at the Cap des Biches. The Valda lozenges company at the edge of town. The Thiwlène neighborhood. Texaco. Mbaye Jacques Diop and Cora Fall, the city's two politicians, eternal rivals. The Matar-Seck lycée.

Bargny. The military engineers' camp, the sentries, the train tracks, the beach. The dreams of exile on that beach. Ndiolmane's bakery. The bridge over the tracks. The trains going to Touba, packed, their only protection the baraka of Serigne Touba. Mr. Fall, Arabic professor, Mr. Ndiaye, schoolteacher and karate instructor. Captain Ndiaye, Polytech graduate, artist and dreamer. Captain Ndione, killed in Guinea-Bissau after stepping on a mine. Tapha Gueye. Phil Collins' *In the Air Tonight.* The courtyard, the mango tree, the garage. My father's blue Peugeot 104. The flowers to water every evening. The sports fields of the military camp. The assault course. The officers' mess. 6:00 p.m., chow time. The Saint Barbara feast of sappers and miners. The drawbridge. The Engineering Training Company: often building, sometimes destroying, always serving. Some conscripts, after three months of training in the hell of Dakar Bango, shaved heads and changed faces, having come for their weapons qualifications. Mass 36, A52, practical range 400 meters, maximal range 1,200 meters, Famas, M16. The school bus. Mr. Malak. Ibou Ndiaye, Ass, Pa Amadou, Cheikh. The Barro's house, Dionewar in the heart of Bargny. The horse and the bit. The city hall, the small square, the mosque. The Baye Peul house. The abandoned train station. The Tabaski and Korité feast days. The killer eight kilometers. The easy eight kilometers.

The Diamniadio junction. The gendarmerie. A little before that, the quarry. Diass, Gandigal, Sindia, then the road to Mbour. At this point in the rainy season, the savannah is green and lush. The paved road seems like a red vein disappearing deep inside the land. The path back to my origins, the ascent to the source. A few lonely baobabs, majestic. The "we" calls out, the "I" yearns for the source and tries to merge into it. The red vein that irrigates the green meadows. The millet sprouts already raising their heads.

Mbour. The main road, the horse-drawn carriages, the teeming bus station. We take the road to Joal. A brief stop-over to say hello. A cousin's lack of enthusiasm. It's often like that when you come back on vacation; few people seem truly happy to see you. We're used to it. We head for Joal. Ngasobil, stone wells, the seminary where Senghor studied for a while. Negro-Africans still pursue their spiritual journey here, only the form has changed.

Mbodiène. I think of Jonathan, my brother in arms, now a legionnaire. It was reported that one day a huge fish washed up on the beach of Mbodiène. For days the inhabitants regaled themselves, feasted and gorged on this gift from the ocean. The result: the good people of Mbodiène were afflicted with such violent diarrhea that the beach was not wide enough to relieve their ravaged intestines. The entire village looked back on this event as a shameful tragedy. Ever since, it is forbidden to utter the phrase "the Mbodiène fish." Do not hold me responsible for what might happen to you if one day, sitting in the shade of the tamarind trees of Mbodiène, your discretion flags and you happen to mention this glorious event. A word to the wise!

The savannah decreasingly green, the baobabs more and more lonely. Then, gradually, the land gives way to the sea. The smell of the Atlantic and dried fish, the first flies and there it is, Joal, *the shade giver.* The Dakar Garage has moved. Reunion with Jules Diouf, joyous. We take the road to Samba Dia and steel ourselves for 25 kilometers of *rang-rang*. A bumpy, pitted track on which the *seven-seater* taking us there weaves its way. Everyone traveling to Djifère dreads the *rang-rang* road.

Fadial and its majestic baobab ringed with masks. Samba Dia. The crossroads. The road to the left leads to Ndiosmone, Ndangane, Fimela. We take the one to the right, direction Djifère. Palms and palmyras, straight and imposing. Then gradually, the tanns, stretches of white sand the sea has receded from. A few pelicans here and there lazing around. The sea water that seeps in, the increasingly persistent smell of the Atlantic. After a dozen kilometers, we reach the first of the Palmarins, Ngounoumane. The men alongside the road are very black, true Serers, formed by the land and the ocean. Then Palmarin Ngeth, Palmarin Mgalou, Palmarin Diakhanor, and finally Djifère. The land ends here. If you want to go any further, you need to brave the sea.

The pirogue that was supposed to come and pick us up isn't here, and it will soon be nightfall. In the port of Djifère, we try to find a pirogue that can take us to the island of Niodior. Negotiations begin. The boatsman looks us over, examines our clothes, analyzes the situation—the late hour, our fatigue, the language we speak, our accent—before announcing a price. He hits hard. We let him know that we are from the area and that we know how much fuel is needed to take us to the island. We finally work out a deal and pay him half of the announced price.

It's dark out. The small pirogue moves across a calm sea. It's low tide as we approach Kooko. In the night we can make out the buoys. If it weren't for the navigational skills of Abdou Fall, we would have run aground on the sandbars. Niodior island is sparkling. We get off on the wharf. The usual rough docking.

Before our arrival at the Boussourra compound, my grandmother is already aware that we are on the island. News travels fast. We stop over in Dinguaré at a phone booth niched inside a house so that I can make a call to France. Silhouettes move around in the darkness, transform the space-time, and the dim light enhances their presence and their solemnity. The owner has guessed who I am. He must have been helped by a few clues, the call to France and perhaps the phenotype of the Sarrs from Boussourra that I wear on my face. Back at the source. Warm greetings. Mama Ami touches me, feels my features, takes in the physical reality of my presence. She says she is pleased that we have come all the way here to see her. Whether we have chosen to live over there or here, the important thing, she says, is that we have not forgotten where we come from. Uncles, aunts, cousins. Old man Saliou has passed on. His room is now occupied by others. One new thing—a television in the courtyard with kids from the compound clustered around. Mama Ndinguane gives thanks to the great shepherd Roog Sène for having protected us. She prays that he will watch over us on land and sea, inside and outside, in the highest places and in the depths of chasms. She reminds us that all suffering comes to an end and counsels us to summon up *mougne,* patience. After dinner it is decided that we will sleep in the Kooko campground.

We take along a few things for the night and cross the bay of Sonaane in a small rowboat. Calm, beauty, poetry. Moonlight shimmering on the sea, mangroves, the soft sound of water lapping. A feeling of boundless peace. An overpowering beauty that seizes your heart. Amadou, my uncle, is at the helm. The weariness of the day melts away. The echo of Europe grows faint. Immersion in the moment. Complete presence in time.

September 19, 2003

A month was enough to get a lot of things done. At the beginning of each autumn, my body recalls the five *Heian*, *Bassai*, *Tekki*, and *Kanku*. It's like the beginning of a new academic term. I put my body to the test. There is no reason that it too should not be *awake*. I need to push its boundaries and be sure that it remembers the forms. At the beginning of the path, one recalls the forms—they are a tool of self-development. At an advanced stage, one forgets them. First up, running in the Valley Stadium. I've been going there assiduously for almost two years now, at all hours of the day. I've become familiar with all its nooks and crannies, the grasses and gravel paths, the cool rose-colored track, the small, wooded footpath, 100 meters long, its squirrels darting out of the thickets, and my pounding, beating heart. The accelerating pulse rate, lungs spewing out the smoke from my smoker neighbors, the self-struggle. To test myself, surpass myself. What's the risk? Physical death. Just a postponed rendezvous.

I love Elignane. Already at her age she manifests strength, temperament, pugnacity, energy. I hope that these times will not corrupt her, instill in her the culture of whining. Strength rarely grows by rubbing shoulders with weakness, which, like an acid, eats away and corrodes it, and slowly diminishes it. Elignane is one year old.

Running, Writing

Running on the east side of the corniche in Dakar. My companions are Abdou Fall, Djiby and Saliou. We look like a combat platoon in training. Running in a group motivates and solidifies and strengthens. Running in a group sets up a shield against the wind pushing us back. Starting point: the Dial-Diop officers' quarters. Then *Clinique de la Madeleine*, the English embassy, *Hôpital Le Dantec*, the former courthouse, the bus terminal, the Atlantic Ocean, the ice cream and drinks sellers, Cape Manuel, Bernard Cove, Terrou Baye Sogui, the Lagon 2. The wealthy young Lebanese on their scooters, the private tennis clubs, Gorée island off in the distance, the brilliant sunlight. The countless athletes, the sand banks, the adolescents playing soccer on the beach with El hadj Diouf and Fadiga jerseys. Hard-played games. Bullying. Insults. Character-building.

Djiby and I are returning from exile. To see clearly, your eyes need to move away. We are observing, seeing this country for the first time. The profusion of colors, voices, smells, laughter, words, enthusiasms, suffering. Profusion is different from dissipation—it is an expansion of generosity. No self-serving calculations here, no microeconomic rationality, no petty acts, no greed. Everyone is invited to the party here, those known and those unknown, next-door neighbors and guests passing through. Beneath this sky, joy does not discriminate, does not partition, is not sparing in its distribution; its recipients are not chosen or elected. It flows to everyone, it is democratic, open, never introverted. Joy is a feeling that can't be locked up—at the risk of stifling it, seeing it waste away. A passion too great to be satisfied by something too confined. The people I am observing practice a spirituality that is immune to everyday concerns. They are perfecting the art of living together. High aspirations passed on by everyone. The daily practice of encouragement. Popular songs and proverbs set a high value on kindness, self-denial, courage and loyalty. Greetings and casual conversations go on for hours. A high degree of socialization, of civility, of civilization. Near the beach, a mother is bathing her child in a basin of water. She scrubs him with a *djampé*: a scrap of fishing net. The soapy water stings the child's eyes. A lesson in roughness, in rigorous cleanliness. No hint of pleasure or relaxation during this shower she makes the child take. Nothing tenuous. The child tries to resist and encounters an admonition: "Sit down and don't move! You don't like it? You're pouting? I don't want to see that look on your face!" It's a bath that opens up, that *unseals*, nothing half-hearted. Relationships are demanding here. Faces are scrutinized, analyzed; the slightest expression is detected. A friend comes to see you: he looks at you, evaluates your physical and psychic condition, tries to hear what you are not saying. A closeness and intensity of relationships. Truth in relationships, truth in speaking, truth face to face. This toughening bath that is African society shapes special kinds of human beings.

The people I am observing have a guileless joy. They have experienced the profundity of mountaintops and abysses. Having experienced the foundations, they are on familiar terms with the summits of humanity. These people, the oldest in the world, have endured. Their joy is not naïve. It crowns a lucidity acquired on the ancient shores of their peregrinations. Have these people lost some of their greatness, some of their glory? They have lived through times when their brilliance was dulled (covered with thin layers of dust). But this is nothing but spume. Their constancy and their *hysteresis* still resonate in their soaring words that carry and enrich their creative force.

These people with their guileless joy, their incisive humanity and their inextinguishable strength, are the African people.

Any people that preserve a living spirituality practice an ascent, a movement upward, a striving toward something better.

Akou Njourel

Yesterday I met up with Modou. He was dressed in Baye Fall[3] clothing and was singing *khassaïdes* in the streets of Dakar. I was very surprised to see him like this. The last I had heard he was working in a bank. I recalled that his father was a pious man, a devoted Mouride. But that didn't explain this. Even more surprising was when I told him I had come to Senegal on business, he replied that he had become a musician and was playing in a group. There was nothing in his career path that could have predicted such a future. He was a brilliant student at the lycée and distinguished himself in his university studies in Bordeaux, and then *quickly* returned to Senegal. After all, why should a life path have to be consistent? People of his generation had been taught this. From the first years of lycée, students knew that if they wanted the maximum number of options at the university, they had to complete a degree in the sciences. A career path had already been laid out for them and included either enrollment in a university or preparatory classes for entry into one of the prestigious Grandes Écoles—Ponts et Chaussées, Mines, Centrale, HEC, or l'X—which would lead to an executive position, preferably in a multinational corporation that did business in Senegal. The sons of government officials, doctors, military officers, and teachers, they came from the upper middle class, and all went to the same lycées. Their families paid close attention to their studies, and they were all there during graduation ceremonies, beaming with pride at their success. Their achievements were ultimately a family affair. They may not have been the most talented of students, but their families had found a way to shape them, to mold them like clay, and to pass on a fervent will to succeed. They were the extensions of their families' hopes and ambitions, and a new life lived through them offered a second chance. It enabled the parents to make up for mistakes and missteps, wipe away their failures and bad luck. This terrible coercion resulted in many thwarted destinies, stifled talents and wasted lives. And the crime was even more heinous since it was cloaked in the mantle of love, and education, and passed-down wisdom. The emasculation began at an early age with the idea that a child was always obliged to honor his parents, make them proud and never question their wishes. If the child didn't abide by the rules, his parents' disapproval would hover over his life like a malevolent shadow that would cause the ruin of all his life projects. In Wolof, the term is *Akou Njourel*, which can be translated as "birth debt."

Birth was such a huge debt children owed their parents. They had been given a gift so precious that if they dishonored it by not fulfilling all their parents' desires, they would be seen as thankless, cursed and wretched. Hence the normal failures and challenges of a lifetime were blameworthy in advance: "You are experiencing these misfortunes because you opposed your parents and it's their *Akou Njourel* that is raining down on you!" Nice trick. The parents had experienced, seen, felt, and known everything that life could teach. "No matter how high the blow, the head will always be above it," as the proverb says. To which Wilhelm of Saxony retorts, with resounding laughter: "A toothless mouth hath no longer the right to every truth."

The dominance and omnipresence of tradition. Children here are beings stuck in a repetition loop. There is nothing new that they can grasp on their own. No new experiences, no novel situations that the parents are unaware of, and, consequently, they have nothing to learn from their children. In brief, nothing new under the sun. The laws of the past rule the present, the genius of young generations is negated, the cult of continuity reigns supreme. One good aspect of the tradition of *Akou Njourel* is the preservation of the respect and esteem owed to the elders. They are not tossed into old folks' homes to die in their autumnal years, and there is a sense of gratitude and appropriate recognition that are expressed through this tradition. We are never born alone. We owe our growth and survival to the care lavished on us when we were young and weak. A certain sense of honor forbids us from closing the door through which we arrived, that once we are satisfied with our lives, we don't forget how we got there. A negative aspect: servitude, the tyranny from which you can free yourself only by paying a price. And the price to pay is disconnecting, cutting the cord. Modou had paid the price. He had been programmed from an early age to become an "important man" of this country. Good schools, consistent, serious studies, competitive spirit. One evening, during a conversation about the many years that had passed since we last saw each other, he told me that each time he ended up first in his class, his father never expressed any satisfaction. He would simply point out that the class was weak and that in the country of the blind, the one-eyed man was king. At this time, his father, a Prefect of the Republic, was traveling through all the regions of Senegal. He would say to Moudou: "We'll see in Dakar if you'll still be first in your class!" It was his way of urging his son to reach higher and further, to be his best. Modou's father had a method for everything; he was a complex, enigmatic man. He had found a way to look after his family, the children of his late brother and his extended family who had remained in the village, with great generosity and an elevated sense of sacrifice. Modou was the third son of his father's brother, but he had only known one father and called him *Nfa*. People close to the family knew that he was in fact his nephew, but no one else ever suspected it. It was only later in life that Modou would learn of this side of his story. Modou's father had instilled in his children and those of his brother a strong work ethic, self-sacrifice, integrity and commitment to community. Such values were sufficient for the life of a man, but, alas, through an unfortunate excess of zeal, he was also determined to shape "great men." The mission he had set for himself was to be a *shaper of destinies*. Who knows why or from where this ambition came to him. He was successful in his own life and had shaped his own destiny. But it seemed like that was not enough for him. He wanted to create an empire, to found a dynasty, to prolong his life's work, and his ambitions—and one life was not enough to do so. He needed other bodies into whom he could infuse his own spirit and dynamism. And Modou was an ideal candidate. This government administrator who had spent his career managing the masses, working at the heart of the apparatus of command and control that comprises the State, had thought a great deal about his strategy and was convinced of its effectiveness. He believed in determinism, in the virtues of the mold, and a methodical approach. The same causes always produce the same effects—just as in a chemistry lab, where a mixture of two substances in the same proportions inevitably produces the same precipitate. For him, man was an animal that could be tamed, molded and formed. *Akou Njourel* was an important part of his domestication project.

One of the first freedoms that Modou mastered was the ability to clearly express his opinions. In Wolof, *soutoura*, a word of Arabic origin, means "discretion" or "modesty." "If there is peace in a community, it is because people know things that they do not say," says the Senegalese proverb. In the country of Kocc Barma and Senghor, a basic tenet of *soutoura* is that not everything that is known is talked about—the neighbors' financial difficulties, people's family problems, etc. This sense of discretion expands to include very minor things. For example, when sitting around the dinner table and an unpleasant odor wafts into the room. Everyone has detected the proprietor of the transmitting anatomy, but no one says anything, or even grimaces to acknowledge the disagreeable smell caused by the foul gas. They put up with it, their faces impassive, and patiently continue the meal as though nothing has happened. Protect peoples' private lives, avoid embarrassing them—in brief, a kind of benevolent discretion. In other latitudes, someone would have had the bright idea to blurt out with a stifled laugh, like on a playground: "Oh no! You farted!"

Unfortunately, the gerontocracy transformed this sense of discretion into an instrument of power. The society of *soutoura* became a society of insinuation, of the unspoken and hidden, of hypocrisy. *Soutoura* requires that not all truths be spoken out loud (especially to the elders). Power relationships are condensed into the ability to speak, which is reserved for a minority, the eldest. This pretext affords a substantial gain for the art of conversation and universal civility, and the art of nuance reached new peaks of refinement. Modou's father, a gifted psychologist, knew how to make deft use of the conversational monologue. During their discussions, he would spell out his views for minutes at a time, without interruption. It was not possible to contradict him. Something in his demeanor made you into the interpreter of his ideas, while yours could only be exposed at the risk of what might appear to be a lack of respect. The father was a master of prolepsis. He would give you the illusion of being engaged in a dialogue, but in fact would anticipate, and then refute, any counterargument you might put forward. His posture, and a certain sense of decorum, tended to disarm you and make you abandon what you wanted to say. He would anticipate your objection and quash it before you could even find the words. Prior to his self-exile, Modou had become, out of necessity, a master of *resumption following silence.* He would listen attentively to his old man while waiting for the moment when his sentence was about to come to a full stop. It was in this brief respite at the end of a sentence, which might last no longer than a pause or a half-sigh, that Modou would stealthily slip in his stream of words. In this way he was able to say a few words without committing the crime of lèse-majesté and interrupting his father. Faced with such an imposing opponent, Modou himself had become adept in communicative strategies. He had had to hone his skills in listening, positioning, and clearly formulating his ideas while smoothing over any aspects that might cause offense and avoiding ambiguity so that others couldn't pretend to not understand what he was really trying to say. Nuances, subtleties, refined speech, hard-hitting expressions that stopped short of being shocking. Right up to the time he left, this was how communications with his father took shape, and he was often at a disadvantage because his father had the prerogative of ending the discussion whenever he liked—preferably after a long, educational, injunctive tirade that set forth his vision of the world conclusively.

In the early days following his return from exile, and despite the euphoria of reunions, Modou sensed that they were keeping a close eye on him. Had he lost his way? Had he embraced Western values to the detriment of good African values? Had he lost his faith, his sense of family belonging, his respect for the elders? But the doubts of those first days faded and gave way to a collective joy. Everyone was happy. The prodigal son had returned with a good diploma, found a job in a good bank, wore a suit during the week and a boubou on Fridays, and after a few months had begun to make additions to the family home. He was the archetypal Senegalese success story. Uncles, aunts, neighbors, the whole neighborhood showered him with blessings and sang his praises. He was the son that everyone would have liked to have. And to crown it all, he knew how to talk to them. His smooth, shimmering words made their hearts beat faster. He would also slip them a few crisp bank notes on occasion—and there was no lack of occasions: births, deaths, tabaski, korité. *Mashallah!* He's so well-mannered that boy! *Ndeysaane!* He's so kind-hearted! *Laabir!* Let's hope he stays that way, may God preserve him from *Chaytan*, from the evil eye and forked tongues!

In the neighborhood, mothers made thinly veiled offers of their clearly unveiled daughters in marriage. Everyone was relieved. Modou effortlessly returned to his society, his home and his role, like a brick slipped back into place in a building. It was as though all the years of exile hadn't left the slightest trace in him. Modou understood that he needed to take advantage of this state of grace before the noose tightened again permanently—this brief period when everything could be restored, relationships renegotiated, the social contract rewritten because it had been deferred for so long—so that he could spread the word that he was no longer exactly the same person, that he had become *himself* and that from now on they would have to accept him as he was. Urban languages are more prone to vacillation, to convoluted speech. The city is seductive and tempting, a prostitute who arouses all desires. Men from all over converge there to suckle at her breast. Her language is sweet and syrupy. Modou decided to go back to using Mandinka—a language forged in the rocks of the countryside—to speak his truths, and to using French to create a certain distance. Expressions like "I disagree" and "That is out of the question" cropped up in his speech, spoken calmly and forcefully. He didn't smoke in the living room, out of respect for his parents, but he did in the courtyard, in full view of everyone, and he rarely joined in group prayers. Then, one morning, he stayed in bed. He had submitted his letter of resignation the day before to the office of the director of the CBAO, the bank where he was working. His friend Gomez had discreetly found a small room for him to rent in the Gueule Tapée neighborhood, near Soumbedioune Bay. He left the chic, residential neighborhood of Point E to move into this teeming suburb.

Enola Gay dropped "Little Boy," and this was his family's Hiroshima. He's forsaking a gift from God! He's deserting his post as a respected and well-paid banker to become a musician!

Soubhanallah! Good God almighty! His family didn't understand or pretended not to. They sought the counsel of marabouts. It was rumored that his success had made some people jealous and they had cast a spell on him. He was possessed. At the height of the crisis, his father said of him that if he wasn't possessed, he lacked ambition and was being unrealistic, and that he was a lost cause. His older sister, Mintou, was the only one who avoided the radiation of this nuclear explosion. She wasn't alarmed. She had always known that he would end up like this. She had also found it suspicious that he appeared so perfect and polite when he returned. She said to herself that he was planning something like a velvet revolution. Unlike some immigrants, who as soon as they returned, flaunted their break with tradition through different clothes, or lifestyles, or ways of speaking, Modou was preparing to checkmate in three moves. First, move the knight two squares forward. Reassuring return, satisfy the family, show them that their efforts have not been in vain by offering them time to enjoy their son's success such as they defined it. Second move, bring out the queen. He had always hoped to return his parents' generosity once he was able to do so, to care for them in their old age, become the shepherd of his shepherds. Although they were not in need, he had created a portfolio of securities for them—low-risk investments that would provide them with a regular income for several years. That way they'd be able to afford some trips to other parts of the world and pay for his younger brothers' education. Third move, bring out the bishop and fly calmly away towards his artistic (human) destiny. Checkmate.

The familial Hiroshima lasted for several years, during which time they used every means possible to try to make him change his mind. *Akou Njourel*, persuasion, pity, guilt trips, emotional blackmail—but nothing worked. He got a band together and started, with difficulty, to give some concerts. When distant family members asked for news of him, they would always say that he had been a brilliant student of finance, that he was a banker now, and taking a break and doing a little music. They held on to the hope that the harshness of an artist's life would bring him to his senses. But deep down, everyone had always known. At first, he was allowed to develop his artistic inclinations. Around the time of his adolescence, they stopped encouraging these impulses. This was the age, it seemed, when young people lost their heads, when they gave themselves over to youthful passions, and when, because they lacked experience, they ventured off in dangerous directions. They needed to ensure a more solid success story; the path he was on was too risky, too chaotic, and they couldn't allow him to lose himself on it. But he was an adult now, so what could they do? They weren't going to put him in chains! Little by little, they got used to the idea and they all resigned themselves to accept his new life. And then once his musical career started to take off, they would speak of him in more glowing terms. Besides, he wasn't just a run-of-the-mill singer—he wrote his own songs. The old man regretted some of the things he had said at the height of the crisis. As he grew older, he loosened the reins of his desire for control and wanted instead to pass on his life experience, his hard-earned knowledge and strengths. The squabbles of past years were now forgotten and there was no longer any need for clarification. The precious little time left to him demanded such wisdom. Pass it on, hand it down quickly now, so that the younger generations could reach new heights, and a man with outstretched arms could broaden the horizon. There was just one catch. Modou had this strange habit of dressing in the *Ndiaxass* and singing religious songs in the streets of Dakar with the Baye Fall, even though he had nothing to do with them. He had a home, an income, a good education. Really! This Modou was still bad news. Thermo-dynamics—which holds that life must open up and fall into disorder to remain life—and chaos took precedence over order and determinism. Modou had decided not to become a great man of this country, but a man who chooses his own life and destiny. He was no longer the brick fitting perfectly into its designated place in the edifice, but a fish swimming in the perpetually shifting waters of becoming. Moudou found his place. And when we find our place, my dear friend, we become unshakeable. *Bassai!*

Artists

There is something pathetic and distressing in the obsessive desire for recognition on the part of certain performing artists. Love me! Understand me! Feel me! Tell me you love what I do! There is something unworthy in their way of suffering through the lack of recognition, of wanting to be freed of solitude, and of seeking the comfort of the crowd.

An artist alters the sum of what already exists, and from that moment on the world must reckon with him. An artist is a unique, unprecedented voice. I am not speaking of those who simply echo the desires of the crowd. As a child, the artist experienced the world of dreams and collective language. He boomed out and belched along with the vulgar voices. Then he tore himself apart and became the companion of others who tore themselves apart. He molted, and now the ghost of his diminished voice only retains frequencies that are truly his own.

There are moments in concerts when people resonate. For an instant something meshes, harmonizes. The resonance of intimate voices. The singular voice becomes the echo of voices that have been lost and buried by the process of subjugation. But alas, most of the time strident voices clamor and belch.

Artists are like galaxies; from birth, there is redshift and distancing. In this way, their light can illuminate without burning out. Most people do not want to burn. They fear the fires of hell.

Does the evening star complain of its destiny?

Notes, Silences and Flashpoints

There exists a moment of quietus in the night. A dead zone. A time when the city finally falls silent, switches off, slows down, disengages and comes to a standstill. No more cars, no more traffic. During this witching hour, you can hear the breathing of the city at rest. From the window of someone still awake floats a melody that pirouettes, expands, moves along the shift of spectral lines towards red, reaches my ears, and then grows distant. Its frequency dips, elongates, turns blue.

Music makes a tear in space-time. It perturbs and rearranges particles and sound waves. It replaces the existing arbitrary space-time with an atmosphere devoted to the exaltation of people. It reveals some wave lengths, muffles others. Creating this new cosmic order is a magician's work.

Some musics make a crack in space-time, others flute over it; some ululate over space-time, others flatten and dissolve it.

To play music is to choose the moment of silence to break. To compose is to create things of beauty that you can carry along and activate whenever you please—it's the creation of space and of time.

Playing together gives resonance to individual stories; it is a collective creation of a universe whose expansion we control. You need suns, black holes, agglomerating clusters, binding forces, chaos, dissymmetry...

Playing music means not only not adding to the world's brutality but also tempering it through a feeling that is purified and brought to incandescence.

Niominka Bi

In the studio, the bass is booming. Sitting in a black leather armchair, Niominka Bi is listening. Cheikh Tidiane, the sound engineer, is fiddling with the compressors. The beat needs to be heavy. The bass drum and bass root need to sound in unison, bang like a fist. Xuman, Kant and Andère are here to lend their critical ear. Xuman thinks that the music is well mixed. But he's critical of Souleymane's overly rapid *flow* in this piece: "You should redo the voice pick-up, lay down the text better, articulate the words and make them resonate. Souley, the community needs to listen. This text is beautiful and *conscious*; we need to be able to hear the meaning right from the beginning. Focus on the substance, not the form!" Niominka Bi listens, then nods in agreement: "You're right, in some passages I put more stress on the vocals and voice effects. Maybe we need fewer words in a measure, it's not about boring people with tricks. Let's do another take." Andère is quiet. Niominka Bi looks at him and waits for his reaction. He says nothing. Is his silence a sign of agreement?

He thinks back to his beginnings, when he was singing with his first group. He would often have good musical ideas, and he would then wait for his friends' opinions and hope for their approval. Some of them would say nothing and he found the silence oppressive. It was a silence that refused to recognize his talent. He had often heard that silence in the music world. It tried to disarm and discourage you, nip your talent in the bud, make you doubt yourself so that you give up trying to express yourself. At first, it had a profound effect on him; he couldn't understand such petty-mindedness in people who claimed to be seeking the light. An artist is a sensitive soul and can be easily wounded. Later, he had learned to resist this silence, to shut out its influence, to trust in his own sensibility. And he had also moved past his illusions about artists. There were very few in whom esthetics and ethics, beauty and truth commingled. You had to remain strong on the path of artistic truth. Be sensitive, of course, but become strong and indestructible.

He could sense that Andère's silence was one of quiet approbation. Kant spoke: "Souley, you're being stubborn. I told you to make a club version of this piece. What's your problem? For twenty years you've been holding out against the record industry and the idea of going *commercial*—four quality albums and what have we got to show for it? We can barely feed our kids. We'll give them a track that will be a hit in the clubs, the radio stations will play it over and over, and the rest of the message will get through. What do you have to lose? It's the trojan horse strategy and it's the only way to deal with the system. Plus, what's wrong with making people dance? Rhythm is life!" Souley thought again about the genesis of this song, which was dedicated to Faye. Her life was one of generosity and courage. The song was about moral strength, and he hoped that its infinitely tender words would reach the heavens. Should he chop them up to make a club version? Get the crowd (the pack) writhing and shaking to this song? Kant was not entirely wrong, and it was true that he had been loyal to him for nearly twenty years now. His razor-sharp skank had survived all the ups and downs of their musical adventure. Many session musicians, initially attracted by his already great reputation in the Bordeaux region and in the music scene, had given up on him along the way when they saw that international fame was not coming. It was inevitably the same routine. At first, they would throw themselves body and soul into the project. Then, little by little, feeling that they had now secured their place as musicians, they would become demanding, nitpicking over details, knowing that if they were sacked the whole band would have to rebuild musical chemistry with others, and that this would take time. Raise the stakes, blackmail, hold the band hostage. From his years in the army, Niominka Bi had retained a sense of resilience. Be there and carry on, the soldiers had taught him. In the early days, he had a hard time separating himself from a session musician, but over time, whenever one of them started down that path, he would unceremoniously kick him out of the band. No musician was irreplaceable. Cemeteries were full of indispensable people, and someone else would come along to fill in the *life* position left vacant. He had learned through experience that after some brief moments of doubt, the new recruit would bring a fresh impetus. The music was strengthened and deepened by the newcomer's experience. He was now working on his fifth album, and he dearly wished that this one would *work,* so that he could finally move beyond the hand-to-mouth existence he had endured for so long. Andère had repeatedly told him that commercial success was not important. What mattered was to create a piece of work that lasted, that would both move and emancipate the listener. The road there should not be determined by material concerns. Poetry was a stop along the way, the noblest of them all. Since when should the superior be sacrificed for the inferior? Not giving in to the demands of the entertainment industry, to reducing a work of art into a consumable, disposable object, was difficult, but not impossible. Julien Gracq, Fela, Kundera, Miles, none of them compromised themselves and yet they were not regulars at the soup kitchen. But then, there is being constantly worried about money matters, forcing your family to do without, and dealing with the small hassles that make daily life difficult and affect the happiness of people you love. Not everybody found their bliss in an ascetic lifestyle. Even some of the greatest had to compromise their art to make a living at some point—commissioned operas, plays and farces to entertain kings and princes. Even Uncle Nesta gave them "Could You Be Loved." Didn't the quest for a body of work require this kind of sacrifice, a little scrap of meat tossed to the hounds? Maybe that's what it meant to be mature: paying the price to continue your work. Strategy, endurance. Thicken your skin, resist the forces of standardization, find your fighting spirit. Comfort dulls creativity, they say. But still, a good studio at home, working in peace, freeing yourself from material worries, devoting most of your time to bringing beauty to life with your own hand. Could he afford the luxury of being an *artiste maudit*? He was neither a person of independent means nor from the bourgeoisie, and he had a family back home who depended on him. People like him carried a dual responsibility; first, the survival of the clan; then, the grace of the clan itself and the weight of its poetry. Since beauty has no price, poets can't be paid. Some eras allowed them to live in dignity, others let them starve to death. Once the poetic vocation took root, one had to find the means to deal with material questions; otherwise, the peace of mind necessary for creativity would be destroyed. Just a part-time job, something that wouldn't take all his time, that was the price to pay for independence. And yet, his only real compensation was music. The worries during soundchecks. Will the sound be right? Will there be an audience? Will they embark on the journey with us? And in the end, when the vibe was there and the spaceship flew off towards the infinite, what a feeling of peace! What happiness! What vastness! Such moments vindicated all the hard knocks of his artist's life, and he emerged from them drained and revived by the embrace of beauty.

While Niominka Bi was lost in his thoughts, another monologue was unfolding in the room. Andère had returned to his private thoughts. Of course, he could understand Souleymane's desire for triumph and success. It wasn't exclusively tied to material questions. Moreover, once he realized that the quid pro quo required by the times was a kind of self-debasement, he had, for a while, abandoned the idea altogether. And then success in itself had no value. Whenever second-rate artists achieved success and it was not exclusively a recognition of quality, it lost its meaning. And yet, things weren't so simple. Success was sometimes a mark of value. In that case, it was the deserved recognition of a body of work, of conviction and talent, of courage and a contribution to a collective endeavor that was coming to fruition through the artist. It was also a path for *striving* that appeared in the fog. But most of all, Souley wanted success because it also had the virtue of silencing both true and false skeptics. Deep down, he didn't really care about true skeptics. He wasn't out to prove anything. On the other hand, the false skeptics surrounding him, who knew his talent (his worth) but refused to acknowledge it out of pettiness, jealousy, rivalry, or a desire to drag him down, were now compelled from the outside to grudgingly acknowledge his qualities. He knew that the desire to silence his detractors was a weakness on his part. Seeking recognition from discerning eyes was also a weakness. To win over others, to seek victory, is just one of many circus games. But during game time, we still strive to win, even if we know that it's only a game. We learn to allocate means to ends. The group learns to refine its economy and expand its capacity. This desire for victory is one of the motors of the human adventure. In the silence of his private musings, Andère was thinking that the path to freedom consisted in rising above such concerns. The pursuit of fame and glory was fundamentally trivial. On the path towards the light, this desire had to be tossed aside. Work in silence and in depth, in the shadows if necessary. Vanquish and accomplish, without being triumphant. Triumph over the triumphant. There are victories that do not blaze, just as there are embers that give off heat even beneath their blanket of ash. In art, basing one's life on the pursuit of media success means basing it on something hypothetical, something that depends on trends, the culture of an era, its perceptions, its desires and needs. But above all, it means depending on the desires of others. This is the height of alienation. To live and exist only through the desires of others is the opposite of the act of freedom that art embodies. True glory consists in cultivating beauty. When encountered, beauty converts all souls and gently compels them to rapture.

Quranic Meditations

The voices that still rise up, the ones that say: "Move away! There
are no peaceful meadows or streams here. Illusions, lies. These
daffodils are fake; these brambles are toxic!" Yet here, I find beauty.
Ephemeral perhaps, but radiant. The murmurs of laughter in
the garden next door, the voice of Billie Holiday marking the
rhythm of time, the fading twilight. I am a man of the middle,
of the between-times. My peace resides at the threshold of dawn
and night. Small consolations? Perhaps. The large green book,
the small white one that questions it. These voices that rise up
and intermingle, this cacophony. The peace deep in my soul that
silences all these disputes. The peace of the middle. The turmoil
is only on the surface. Dive down to the depths.

Rumi tells me that I resemble an embryo living in darkness, feeding on blood, and feeling at home in this murky,
viscous pool. If you tell this embryo that outside there is a
sky, an earth, stars and gardens, it won't believe you. Darkness
has little imagination. This world is the feeding trough of the

carnal soul, but the spirit finds no nourishment in the stable. He tells me to flee this world, to die to this world, and to be reborn in the One. To aspire to the source of all bliss and not be satisfied with imitations.

Gibran, for his part, thinks that the master of rhyme has constructed a perfectly rhymed poem. The beauties of this world reflect those of the world above—and so there is no reason to flee them here below. Stig Dagerman whispers to me that although he has rarely encountered consolation, beauty, when it seizes him, transcends time. A single second and an eternity become the same. Our actions, he says, must not be placed on the chopping block of time. Happiness that abides or that is fleeting—false debate. Peace freezes time, pain makes it flow. For Schopenhauer, suffering is the principal argument against existence. The sum of pleasures felt by man over the course of his life does not compensate for the pain he experiences.

No matter how much man struggles or connives against pitfalls and burdens and abysses, he'll still end up being defeated by death, says the man from Frankfurt. And if man struggles, it is not so much out of love for life as it is fear of death, he thinks. Rumi retorts that pain is a blessing. It allows me to call out to Him in the night. And his response is my call. Pharaoh did not have the privilege of pain; it would have allowed him to call to Him. *Labbayka* (I am here) is in the call. It is a blessing that we are allowed to call to Him. He adds that what *is* has no value, but what should be does. Standing before the One is what gives value to man.

Within Rumi's words is an eschatological justification for suffering. To protect against forgetting, he creates suffering. Man remembers only through pain; pain calls for consolation. Isn't giving this meaning to suffering one of the oldest ruses of a humanity incapable of alleviating it?

Pharaoh was struck by pain when the ten plagues befell him, and it was his pride that prevented him from calling out to Him. Out of pride, Satan refused to bow down before Adam. He was damned. One day he said to Moses: "When God asked you to open your eyes and behold the burning bush on Mount Sinai, if you had closed them, you would have seen him."

Tearing away the veil of illusions, facing reality, experiencing loss is always painful (we had believed in acquisition). Isn't hardship the path towards self-knowledge, a necessary stage of one's own evolution? The reality over which we draw the veil only appears to us after pain has shown us the loss of our illusions. Isn't it preferable to accept suffering as an unavoidable reality that is instructive and consubstantial with life? Just as we accept the inevitability of a sunset.

God or Man-God

I am no longer convinced that the universe is the child of the *fiat*. Nor am I convinced of the contrary. I will wander for a long time between these two *countries* until the *Yaqeen* pays me a visit. Throughout my life, faith has provided a direction, a meaning to my actions. It has lifted me up, shaped me, given me a spine. Then gradually it fell apart like a rose mat, unraveled by philosophers, writers, astrophysicists, self-observation, and introspection. I understood the human need for metaphysical and moral comfort, the necessity to curb despair, to keep death at bay. (Faith as a psychological need, deeply rooted in the human psyche). The first moments of this discovery were difficult ones. I was set loose in a world with no reference points or meaning. *Away from all suns.* Everything was possible, everything was now permitted. A world whose disillusionment disoriented me. All my ethical and moral foundations were shattered. The motivations for my actions became grains of millet in quicksand. The world, history and civilization appeared to me to be the result of a will to power. Life, as the desire for existence and survival. Napoleon and Saint Francis of Assisi as two sides of the same coin. And yet, within this chaos of uncertainty where I was staggering along, something awakened inside me. Some unexplored recesses of my being were touched by sunlight, and something new was blossoming, growing, opening. The precariousness gradually faded away, and I realized that life could have a meaning regardless of whether or not God existed. Humans could become adults and establish an immanent ethics—a kind of elegance and benevolence in their relationship to the world. There was no need for the support of any kind of faith. They could rid themselves of their will to order and power. But I was missing the strength that the practice of faith provides. And having definitively chosen the camp of strength, I needed faith like a warrior needs armor—no matter the material, as long as it held firm. In that respect faith was effective; it provided inner strength.

Mysteriously, each time I was illuminated by a sudden sense of the infinite and attempted a return to faith, my life improved. Providence and grace reappeared in my life. What to make of this? When you walk toward me, I run toward you! Or was it my interpretation of events that made me think that? Could I experience the divine without it corresponding to any reality?

Faith freed me from people and their bondages. But I couldn't think of it simply as an effective tool, especially since it stemmed from the conviction of its truth. For some time, I played a kind of fool's game: convincing myself of my faith so that my faith would give me strength. But eventually, I abandoned this game. Yet at the same time I decided to remain constant to Muslim culture and its ethics, out of loyalty to what it had given me in the past, out of loyalty to the spirit of community it had fostered, out of loyalty to my family who embraced it, out of loyalty to its wells of light. I also decided to remain in a state of questioning, one that was porous and wide ranging, and to never settle on an ultimate truth, savoring the shadows and seeking the light.

The Quran is an immense book. Could it be the product of a single man? It says that if it had been sent down upon a mountain, the mountain would have humbled itself and split apart out of fear of God. I have often had this thought: "And what if Muhammed was simply an author of spiritual texts? A brilliant, inspired writer (I know the myth of his illiteracy), but nothing more than a good author?" We've come across brilliant, profound, dazzling authors; but this text is too immense. The comprehensiveness of the dimensions it encompasses, the soundness of its views, its profound understanding of people, its incantatory power, its premonitions, its vision. Its poetry and prose, its fervors and restraints, its concision and its amplitude. Its mysteries and its shadows. Its multiple layers of meaning: its perpetual capacity to produce meaning, its renewed interpretations. Its polysemy. Its vivifying words, its ethics, its poetics. No, I doubt that a writer, even a great one, could conceive such a work in twenty-three years, or even in a single lifetime. A corpus developed by several generations of authors? This text requires a profound knowledge of biblical events, of points of ancient eschatology needing correction. It demands a deep understanding of social psychology, of the human soul and body, of geology and astronomy, of the various human and natural sciences. Through its syntagmatic character, its patterns that intertwine and recur like in a Mongolian rug, this text is too immense. As in all sacred texts, it has something infinitely greater to it, something one doesn't find in the other great texts that human civilization has produced. The sacred texts crystallize in their core the longing for the divine of many generations of human beings. This greater something that cannot be grasped through a solely rational and critical reading. The flow that, beneath the surface of the text, speaks to deep intuition, beyond the intellect. The emotion that was felt by those who first received these words within themselves. The relationship to this text is a matter of sensory experience. Its mystery continued to challenge me...

Then, one day, I met the people of remembrance. They established a relationship with God that was beyond any bargaining or psychological need. A relationship that did not meet any needs, or answer to any fear, anguish, or desire. The explanation of faith as an anthropological need, as simply the fear of finitude, or the desire for security, went up in smoke. These people had preserved the space of the divine from any personal projections. Reality, when contemplated by a heart purged of pettiness, was as obvious as the sun. The people of remembrance left behind the zone of the apparent multiplicity of phenomena and sailed towards primordial unity. Cut from the reed bed, far from their source, their souls were homesick for the primal fusion and yearned for the moment when they would again be united with the Lover. Having attained the *Yaqeen*—the certainty of mystics who have seen God and no longer believe—they possessed a direct and intuitive knowledge, beyond dialectics and formal truths: a knowledge that was vision. I understood that to approach the divine by accumulating erudite knowledge on the subject was a fruitless undertaking. The aim was not accumulation but transformation. When he met Rumi, Shams of Tabriz cited a verse by Sanai: "If knowledge does not liberate the self from the self, then ignorance is better than such knowledge." The divine only revealed itself through a direct point of union, through experience. Contemplation, the sudden beauty that stupefies you, the ecstatic state, and prayer were among these experiences.

The ritual prayers that we perform when we are physically exhausted have always been problematic for me. Worship through the body and the spirit when neither one is present. Convocations at a prescribed hour of the day. Ceremonies of worship devoid of fervor or contemplation, when fatigue creeps in and the yearning for elevating the fragment of the divine within is missing. Or is it simply the effort to worship through one's body, the physical courage, the willingness to make a sacrifice to faith, that counts. "If you cannot see him, know that he sees you," say the expounders of fear and servility. And now we see that for the people of remembrance any act performed in the memory of God is prayer. Because of course, my friends, one day you will have to stop performing the *salat*[4] simply out of fear of hell. Just as one day we stop doing our homework solely out of fear of the teacher, having understood the benefits of broadening our minds and acquiring knowledge. Although in the Muslim tradition the categorical imperative of the *salat* allows for no exceptions, even during times of war, it is essential to understand that this practice must lead to an enhanced quality of the lived moment, to a liberation from the tyranny of fleeting moments, and to a heightened spirituality. A morality of laziness, of negligence? No, an ethics of meaning. "Righteousness does not consist in turning your faces towards the east or towards the west." When you become friends with someone, your relationship develops beyond conventions. You show up at your friend's house unannounced (at least in some parts of the world). And above all, you visit him whenever you want to see him. Spiritual life cannot be boiled down to the cultural practices of a given religious tradition. Reading, thinking, meditating, painting, singing, practicing an art are all acts that, through consecration, immortalize. Any action involving self-presence, a meditative dimension, deep attention, or an immersion in the cosmic flow is by nature spiritual (transcendent). Books, theaters, music halls, dojos are all places where we can forget our tyrannical egos. By abandoning our egotistical self, we make peace with ourselves. We discover our true nature and begin to awaken the inner sleepwalker. Unfortunately, fools will always find a way to turn a mosque into a urinal. There's no end to them. After all, didn't they survive the flood? Our lot to live with them. They are part of the whole and sometimes allow the light to shine through.

Laye

Carnot street is waking up. First horns honking, a fine drizzle that dries on the sidewalks. The Lebanese grocer at *Au bon accueil* opens his store. The *Villa Rose* is shuttered, still submerged in the night's torpor. Maids in headscarves sweep in front of the houses and end up sweeping the whole street. Laye, the shop keeper, has arrived very early this morning. As always, he opens his shop, cleans it, takes out the bench, brings the sacks of bread inside and turns on his radio, which he has tuned to Radio France Internationale. The Americans continue bombing Kunduz and Kandahar. They haven't given up on forcing bin Laden out of his caves. Some NGOs are trying to deliver urgently needed humanitarian assistance to the affected populations. Abdoulaye wondered how these Muslim populations still had the strength to keep the fast amid their ordeals. How could they go on trying to elevate themselves through asceticism and meditation while being bombed, deprived of everything, and struggling to stay alive? All day long he thought about these innocent people being killed in the effort to reach Osama bin Laden. It was not a very busy day, and since it was the month of Ramadan, the city was moving in slow motion. People would come to buy his entire supply of bread a few minutes before the breaking of the fast. Today he was really feeling the effects of hunger. Those last five minutes before the break were particularly long. And yet he refused any self-pity. His ordeal was nothing compared to the Afghans who were spending this Ramadan beneath a shower of bombs. Ramadan was the time to take stock of one's ethics. A time to meditate, to elevate oneself, to redress one's minor shortcomings, to show patience and endurance and compassion. A time to read the Quran, deepen one's understanding of it, meditate on it as though it had just now been revealed, attempt to put its truths into practice. Ramadan was also a time to rediscover the pleasure of meals, a feeling worn away by the daily routine of food wolfed down on the run. The first ten days of the month, the days of horses, had passed by quickly, like they do every year. The ten days of donkeys were just beginning. The fast became more arduous during this period and the days seemed longer. The month would end with the ten days of camels, the final days, and they would pass by very slowly, like tortoises in the desert. After the meal, Laye felt his strength return and his lethargy dissipate. The Americans were still bombing Kunduz and Kandahar. He got up and prepared to say the prayer of the *Maghreb*. He had always loved the twilight, the interval between shadow and light, the gateway to the night. He felt his strength returning. Night fell quickly. The twilight, like a hurried blessing, disappeared. Little by little, Carnot Street came back to life. The fasters who had gone without tobacco all day long lit their first cigarettes on the doorsteps. The coils of white smoke spiraling upwards looked like little Milky Ways as the night grew dark. There was laughter, snippets of conversation, televisions blaring in the background. The muezzin of the El Hadj Malick Sy zawiya was already clearing his throat and calling believers to their faith. Laye tidied up his cantine, cleaned it, brought the bench inside, locked the door and went out. He headed for the port to catch one of the *cars rapides* that went to Thiaroye-sur-Mer.

Thiaroye. A suburb of Dakar on the road to Rufisque. In 1944, a platoon of Senegalese infantrymen were massacred there by the French army for having demanded their back pay. These same soldiers had spilled their blood for France during the two world wars. Sembène Ousmane made a film based on this incident, a film that was banned in France for over a decade. At this late hour, the streets of this working-class neighborhood were overflowing with people. Food stalls were open, kids were playing in the streets, adolescents gathered around a teapot on the doorsteps, lively discussions. Greetings, loud voices, dimly lit alleyways, silhouettes. At times, the calls to prayer from different mosques blended with and echoed one another. On this evening the road to Rufisque was uncongested and Laye arrived home early. He'd be able to perform the *nafila*[5] in one of the neighborhood mosques. His wife Astou, as she did every evening, asked him to have dinner before going to pray. And like every evening, he declined, preferring to eat after he returned for fear that the meal would weigh him down and make him lazy.

After the prayer, Laye lingered inside the mosque and meditated. He had come to understand that as he increased his ethical commitments, he could not help but perceive more acutely the moral degeneration of the society in which he lived. He was profoundly shocked by this, and he felt the intolerance growing in him. He sensed that to better accept his peers, he needed to relax his strict demands—so that by learning to be more lenient with himself, he would be so with others. But this option left him dissatisfied. He thought of this verse from Attar: "Intolerance prevents man from worshiping God." How could one be demanding of oneself while at the same time fully accepting others as they are? How to avoid falling into a pretentious self-righteousness, conscious of one's supposed superior virtue? Perhaps wisdom is knowing how to accept the chaos without complacently wallowing in it. The key must be something along those lines—accept the multiplicity, the nightingale's song, shea butter, the swamps and the lotuses, the cow dung and the brightness of Sirius. After several hours of meditation, he returned home and turned on the radio. On RFI, the news was the same. The Americans were still bombing Kunduz and Kandahar. The commentators were talking about five tons of bombs dropped in a single day and going into raptures about the strike force of the B52s, all of which had returned to their base safe and sound. They were predicting a short war and the imminent capture of Osama bin Laden.

Be Faithful to an Idea
That Elevates You

Shun vanity. Kill off the play-acting in yourself.

See yourself as you are, unflinchingly, without affectation without self-flagellation. From there, use each moment to elevate yourself.

Be good company. Be one of those who spread joy and peace around them, in the air. Those whose presence graces Time.

Know how to accept misunderstandings about yourself.

Never beg. Not for love, nor tenderness, nor understanding. Be free from the approval of others. Never give in to any pressure, however gentle it may be. Be free from the disapproval of others.

Don't rush. Flow with Time, merge with it. Dig beneath the surface. Strive and grow with Time. No toadying, no flattery, no pretense, no compromises. No self-justifications. Don't confide. Protect the flame that is growing in the shadows. Protect it from prying eyes. Hide yourself. The stone lies hidden in the mine to become a diamond. Achieve a victory each day, however small. Kill off Narcissus. Kill off the Clown. Kill off Ubu.

God is an idea that elevates.

Open Forests, Dark Forests

Following the marked paths is a necessary stage of learning. But there comes a day when every person must pass through his own forest, whether dense or sparse, dark or scarlet. There comes a day when every person must clear his own field, trace his own path. Sow his seeds. Deforest his own forest. Commit his crimes and assume his share of the world's darkness. Chase away a little of his darkness and carry his share of the world's light.

For some this will be the fire of love or loss or misery. For others, the flames of ambition, vanity, weakness, desire, cruelty, pride or solitude. For still others, the sharpened blades of sensitivity, of disaffection, of the quest for inner peace—of shadows and light, of bases and summits.

There comes a day when every person *confronts himself* in the three great places of weakness: the premonition of death, disenchantment, ambition.

There comes a day when each individual faces his own truth.

Démosthène Layi

That morning, around seven o'clock, Démosthène Layi heard the metal shutters of the bar across the street being raised. The lines of a poem that Mansa Waly wrote in 1406 came to mind: "The Sine is my orient, to the east of all the levants, Sinig often comes to me like a dream of days past." Sunlight filtered through the blinds and diffused to illuminate the room. He could hear the street noise, increasingly insistent. He thought that once again he wouldn't be able to begin this day with *a song of thanksgiving in his heart*. He rolled over on his sides several times, stretched out, curled up again and finally decided it was time to get up. But his heart wasn't in it. A sense of dread, the source of which escaped him, was causing a pain in his solar plexus. He remembered Hakagure's advice: "Make your decision in the space of seven breaths." On the fifth breath, he got up. In the bathroom, he gazed at himself for a long time in the mirror, examined the dark circles under his eyes and tried to evaluate his level of fatigue. Not too bad, he thought. There were a few pimples of concern on his forehead but the bags under his eyes were less swollen, and his eyes were not as red as usual. This visual indication was important in that it allowed him to adjust the mental and sensory evaluation of his physical fitness. He had often felt his fatigue like a burning in the back of his eyes, a heaviness in the nape of his neck, or a mental fog. These sensations affected his motivation. But they were often false signs, and he had lived through several days where he turned out to be less tired than he thought. Ever since, he would correct for them by carefully examining his face, working out the precise arithmetic of his physical and psychological state. Drag himself out of bed, let the night go, and approach the new day with a refreshed spirit as though it were the first morning of the world.

Démosthène Layi walked out of the bathroom and up to the attic to welcome inside himself that pillar of words rising from the mists of time. He prepared himself mentally during the minutes preceding the *salat*. He tried to empty his mind of everyday concerns. How many times had he gotten up early in the morning, breathing hard, in a rush, anxious to answer the call of profit, and competition, and social success and ambition? How many times had he gotten up very early, washed up, combed his hair, dressed in his finest clothes to answer these calls, for fear of losing his job, of being left behind, while the call of God left him drowsy? He performed his ablutions using water sparingly and tried to calm himself, slow his inner rhythm, and above all, not to hurry. No more praying while thinking about the bus he might miss. Take his time to speak to God. Break the routine. Find his piety and ardor again. He dimmed the light in the bedroom, spread out the mat, stood up straight and recited the call to prayer that Bilal had resounded with his powerful voice in the first hours of the Revelation. He had fallen into the bad habit of dispatching his prayers mechanically, without reflecting on the meaning of the surahs he was reciting or the gestures he was making. He would sometimes finish reciting the *Fatiha*[6] without truly dwelling on it. Outside, the black thread of night was beginning to distinguish itself from the white thread of dawn. After the *Fatiha* he would recite the Surah of the Daybreak. Above all, he thought, he should pause after each phrase, after each sentence, and meditate on its meaning. He raised his hands to his face and said: "*Allah Akbar.*" He paused after the first verse and meditated on the meaning of Rahmani, the most merciful. He reflected on each verse of the *Fatiha*, which was a revelation; it resonated deeply with him, inflected into multiple meanings. Beneath the old letters there was always a new signification. In addition to the *Fatiha,* he also recited the sura of the dawn and the sura of mankind. Before bowing, he reflected again on the *bismallah*[7] and took the time to recite the three *soubhana rabil el azim,* thinking about their meaning. He prostrated and thought deeply about the three *soubhana rabil el aala* that are recited with the forehead touching the floor. He had then completed one *rakat*[8]. He concentrated on each stage during the second *rakat.* Once he had completed this, he paused and recited the *tashahhud.*[9] He then turned his head to the right, and wished peace on people, on angels, on jinns and on the elements. He turned his head to the left and did the same.

Fatigue

I had been in the grips of an old fatigue, one that went a long way back, like a river flowing back to its source. A fatigue as stubborn as dead skin that couldn't be shed. A fatigue that had plagued me ever since I set up camp by the Loire. No matter how much I slept, conserved energy, struggled against it, tried to rest, nothing worked. I was caught in its grip. My body and mind seemed to be stuck in a quagmire. My entire reality was held hostage by this fatigue that prevented me from reading, working, creating, or thinking. Those rare moments when I experienced a clarity of mind felt like rediscovering paradise. I was weary of always being tired. My will and my desire for work had never been stronger. My resolution to make sparing use of time, to not waste it, to set one stone upon the other in the seconds passing by had never been so tenacious, or so fruitless. I had to get some rest. So, I decided to eliminate anything that was superfluous from my daily occupations and to self-impose a spartan discipline. Get to bed early, exercise, eat well, give my mind a rest whenever it became foggy. After two weeks, I began to come back to life a bit. I was so eager to make up for the lost time that I threw myself back into the work with a relentless frenzy. Then the fatigue brought me down again. Two weeks' time wasn't enough. Then I understood that I needed to act with resolution, and wisely. To rely on duration. To patiently flush the fatigue from my pores, remove each incrustation of it like you would scour the bottom of a pot. To stick to my discipline and not try to do more than I was capable of, even if I was feeling better. Not overdo things. Not give into feeling guilty about doing nothing. No longer respond to every demand on my time. My fatigue concerned me deeply and I quickly realized that I would have to confront it alone, that no one in my circle of friends could help me. They were probably too used to seeing me carry the burdens. I understood that I would need even more courage and will to vanquish this fatigue. It became a question of survival, and I had to take it very seriously. I learned that rest is also a kind of work. I was midway on the path of life, and I felt as though I was at the end of the arc. I was already experiencing my limits.

Sleep, Pre-sleep

The muted anguish upon waking up, as though you were returning from a faraway place, the shadow country. As though you were almost stranded there, like a near-death experience. The post-nap anguish, the brief dive into self-oblivion, as though you were violently pulled back from a mortal danger.

Pre-sleep. The everyday worries rise to the surface, swirl around your mind, then gradually fade away, and you are submerged in the night. The anguish of the first seconds in the void, then the vertigo stops. Darkness.

Failure to dive into the abyss. The everyday concerns won't leave. They prevent your body and mind from sinking into sleep. They keep watch and keep you awake in a state of half-sleep, half-clarity. The vision state.

Alexander Graham Bell

I made a call to Senegal. The news was not very good. Rokhy has been sick for a few days, bedridden with headaches, diarrhea, vomiting, aches and pains. She didn't go to the doctor and tried to treat herself with medicine that was in the house. The old man suggested she go to Kooko with the children to get some rest. They didn't go. I imagine that this is all connected to some passing problem they're not telling me about. Soutoura. I asked her to go see the doctor on Monday; I'll go to the post office tomorrow. I spoke with the old man, and he asked for news about the whole family. Rokhy offered a blessing: may Roog Sène, the great shepherd, watch over us all. That's how it is in Senegal—immersion in the hard reality of daily life. From here, you can choose to be aware of it, or to turn away from it by not asking. Distance reduces the proximity of compassion. You no longer experience the day-to-day difficulties of your dear ones—their illnesses, their hopes, their successes and failures all seem far away. You no longer have an idea of their preoccupations, their longings, their expectations, their fears. Time and distance cut furrows in our souls. Little brothers grow up, girls who were barely pubescent get married and become women. Parents grow old and approach the end of their lives. Time withers. The time to spend with them frays away. For that, Alexander Graham Bell's invention is very useful.

Synchronicities

September 13, 2003. I'm reading *The Belly of the Atlantic* while listening to the Serer diva Yandé Coudou Sène. At the point in the song where she sings: "The lion doesn't like *mboum*, it feeds on meat," I am on page 275 of the novel. Fatou Diome is relating the victory of the Lions of Senegal over Sweden during the 2002 World Cup games and she mentions this song by Yandé Coudou, the one I am listening to at the exact same moment while I am reading this passage. It's an astonishing concurrence. Acausal synchronicity?

I try to think of an explanation. It's likely that listening to Yandé Codou and reading this novel are related things. I've only been back from Senegal for a few days and I'm feeling very nostalgic. Fatou Diome has just published this novel in which she evokes the themes of emigration, exile and alterity. Curiosity and a "fixed passion" for literature compel me to read the book. Yandé Codou, Fatou Diome and I belong to the Serer people. In the end, there's nothing surprising in Fatou Diome mentioning the Serer diva in her book. And yet why, at the very moment when I am listening to this specific song (there are a dozen titles on the record), do I find myself on exactly page 275, the passage where she refers to the same exact song? I do a quick mental calculation and realize that the probability of this concurrence is close to zero (0.00033). So, why?

Nietzsche says that there is a culminating point in life; when we reach it, we are in great danger of intellectual servitude, because our minds are seized by the idea of a personal providence. An idea, he says, that has the best of advocates on its side: the apparent evidence we can observe that everything that concerns us always seems to turn to our advantage. Everyday life seems to prove this proposition. Whatever it is, good or bad, the loss of a friend, a slander, a sprained ankle, a letter that doesn't arrive … All of it appears to us as something that could not *not* have happened, something full of meaning and profound usefulness. He warns against this idea. We must be content to admit that our practical and theoretical skill at interpreting and arranging events has reached its peak, he says. The wonderful harmony produced by the playing of our instrument is too beautiful for us to dare to attribute it to ourselves. In fact, if anyone is playing with us, it is chance. Chance leads us by the hand and "…even the wisest providence could not devise any finer music than that of which our foolish hand is then capable."

So, chance? Nothing but a lovely coincidence? A skillfulness in arranging and interpreting events, according to Nietzsche. I, on the other hand, treasure the idea of a *zaban el hâl,* literally the "language of the spiritual state." Within the Muslim mystical tradition lies the idea that beyond words there exists a direct transmission between spirits of the same nature, between spirits sharing the same quest. A *Pîr*, a spiritual master, upon arriving in a city, communicates directly with the spirits of mystics (contemplatives) who live there, without having known them beforehand. These beings possess an inner quality that functions as a force field that is crucial for the preservation of life. I became convinced that certain spirits continue to communicate across space and time. In the caravanserais of boundless space, they meet and converse. Having freed themselves, they drift across the ether and live inside the light they have finally found. When we approach them, they manifest themselves through encounters of this kind. Souls that swim in the same ocean unite seamlessly. The spirit of Yandé Coudou was present on that day. Through the concurrence of a text and a piece of music, it wanted to deliver a message of courage: "The lion is nourished by meat."

While exploring the thinking of Epicurus, I came across the word "increscescible." I looked it up in one dictionary but couldn't find it. However, I did chance upon the word "increate". I decided to have a look in a different dictionary, which I opened randomly without any reference to the alphabet, and there again I came across the word "increate" (God is increate). Just below was the word "incredulous."

Sesshin

Wednesday, May 24. We arrive in Vichy around 7:30 p.m. Check into the rooms. The old hands show me the way, help me to make my bed and get my bearings. That evening Jean-Paul invites us to a copious meal at a restaurant on the banks of the Allier, the Alligator. He and Vincent take good care of me. A very generous concern before the hammer falls. At 11:30 p.m., a girl walks into the room I'm staying in that has three beds. The concierge made a mistake by putting her in with me. He was probably confused by my first name. I end up in a single room.

Thursday, May 25. I wake up at 4:15 a.m. Around 4:30 a.m., old hands knock on the doors of our rooms. Bare-footed and in kimonos, we go outside into the cool darkness. Feet touching gravel and damp grass. There are about a hundred and fifty of us in a large dojo. Women and men of all ages, from all over, who share in these principles, in the midst of a weakening civilization, come here every year, compelled to engage in this demanding confrontation with themselves. Break through mental blockages, overcome inner resistance, switch to a different regime, rediscover the wellspring of energy clogged by the socialization process. The DTN says a few words about the program and then barefoot jogging on the gravel and cool grass. People energized by breathing, wearing white kimonos, awaken at the same time as the universe, begin again with the dawn. The leading group is compact, with good energy flowing through it. You feel like a piece of cork floating down a stream. Two and a half hours of kiyon. 7:30 a.m., the first training session of the day is over, off to the showers, then to the atrium. Jean-Paul doesn't come to breakfast with us; he's hurt his knee. Back to the rooms. Rest. Lunch at noon. This time three of us go together. Return to the rooms. Rest.

During this break I sleep a little, drink a lot of water and read François Cheng's meditations on beauty. Next training session at 3:30 p.m. 3:30–6:00 p.m., outdoor training. Divided into groups at different levels, intensive *Ten no Kata* and *Bassai*. 9:30–11:00 p.m., *Iai* fighting in the dark. Good sensations. The DTN has informed us about the next morning's difficult session so that we can mentally prepare ourselves, he says. I think it's more so that we will dwell on it all night. I decide not to think about it.

Friday, May 26. Wake up at 4:45 a.m. Barefoot jogging. An hour and a half of *kiba-dachi*. It teaches you a lot about yourself. At one point of the *kiba-dachi*, Jean-Paul comes by to support me with his wounded knee. He stands in front of me, in *kiba-dachi* stance, his eyes boring into mine, and passes on his prodigious inner strength. From his soul to my soul, *ishindenshin*, from his spirit to my spirit, from his body to my body, from his wounded knee to my perfectly healthy knees. After lunch, he debriefs me on the session, 3:30–6:00 p.m., outdoor training. The weather is beautiful. Intensive foot kicks in the *Ten no Kata* style from yesterday. Rhythm. Timing. 7:00 p.m., dinner. 8:00–9:00 p.m., meeting with the senior members of the FSK; they talk to us about their paths and share their experiences. Some of them have completed eighty specialized training courses. I keep company with an old Cameroonian man whom I met previously at the fortieth anniversary in Mulhouse; Master Oshima was there. Despite his advanced age, he never misses a special course. His nickname is the Old Lion. Midnight to 1:00 a.m., a thousand *Oi-Tsuki* in the dark, in hommage to (memory of) the old ones who once had to practice in secret in Okinawa.

Saturday, May 27. Wake up at 5:15 a.m. Barefoot jogging. Katas. At the conclusion of the course, Shodan, Nidan and Sandan awarded. 3:30–6:00 p.m., *Sambon Kumite*, dreaded by all. Learned a lot about morphopsychology, and others, and consequently about myself. Pleased with my session. 9:30–11:15 p.m., *Oi-Tsuki, Gyaku Tsuiki*. The airplane stance, a real torture. Relationships with others. The *Zanshin* spirit. This evening, I triumphed over myself. Tomorrow morning, last training session, eighty katas on the horizon.

Sunday, May 28. Wake up at 4:45 a.m. Jogging. Eighty intense katas. The five *Heian* (ten times), ten *Bassai*, ten *Kanku* and ten *Tekki*. Final training. End of the 2006 special national program. For those who wish to advance in rank, it's not over yet, there is one more session after breakfast. The Old Lion is going to present his Nidan.

During this period, I lived moments of extreme intensity.

September

September arrives. Autumnal pleasures, perpetual rebirth. The unceasing struggles of becoming. Yet my masters of the day tell me to give up wanting to become, and content myself with being. But I cannot extinguish the fires that have been lit. I've been slow cooking this dish for a long time and now I'm ready to serve it. I have finally understood that it was pointless to seek wisdom in high summer. It's the prime of life that clamors for one's force to be scattered and consumed by futile and empty quests Each age has its torments, its moments of grace, its contemplations. Autumn brings detachment, a calming of passions and a serene savoring of life's ephemeral beauty.

I began my account on a day in this gentle month of amber-hued sorrows. That is when my cry broke through. September is January for me. Distant luminescence in a sky whose azure I want to widen, with my arms outstretched to broaden the horizons. I, Fadel, Laye, Modou, Bouba, Singhiam and Démosthène Layi—these are all my possible vistas.

I love new relationships, new cities, new poems, spaces where nothing is determined yet—not judged or prejudiced, no legacy, no background, no balance of power, or of fascination, or obligation, or avoidance or competition. No routine, no certainties. Where you have not yet been walled in by what you are, or what you are supposed to be, or supposed to have been. We experience renewal in such spaces, give voice to other potentials, shed dead weights and lethargies, experience rebirth, and simply *are*.

What have I accomplished over these past years? I have read. I have opened myself up. I have freed myself. I have reconnected with the ancient chain. I have cleared a path.

This morning, the *great teacher* was on again. The end of a random program, Sunday morning on the France 2 channel. Dante on the road to Ravenna. Paradise, which according to Christian eschatology begins with baptism, historically. The idea of eternity imposes a different rapport with the present. Paradise: humanity reconciled with itself. Dante's final verse: the love that moves the sun and other stars.

Love moves the planets; I am sure of it. It's the gravity, the binding force that agglomerated the vagrant clumps into planets following the great separation. It is the patience that distilled energy into matter, the breath that gave it life.

Just a few words to melt the ice. Paradise, time, eternity, love, humanity reconciled. Dante on the road to Ravenna. Dante in exile.

All rivers lead to the sea.

I wandered off in many different directions while writing this book, wondering where to start it, what to say in it. Did I need to tell a story? Should I lend my voices to characters, echo the world's voices? Novel, essay, long poem, fragments, aphorisms, chronicle of passing time, meditations? How to avoid the trap of exhibitionism? How to find a voice without *egotizing*? A book: a mirror space, a space for the quest of self-knowledge, a place to set anchor. I wandered around these questions for a long time. The necessity of a face-to-face encounter with myself was imperative. Writing fulfilled a desire to bring myself together, to collect myself, to realize my unity. Writing responded to an enigmatic imperative. I thought of the works that had transported me without running up against the constant presence of the authorial I. Writing is a paradoxical act of affirmation and annihilation. To say "I" means starting with oneself as the center, it is giving birth to a word that creates a cosmos. "I" is also someone else whose spirit moves through me, the other I have listened to and understood, the other whose intimacy I inhabit, the *alter* whose surges of feeling and passions I have embraced. To say "I" is a self-affirmation; but it is also a self-dissolution, a self-obliteration.

On several occasions I let this narrative lie fallow. When I would return to it, I sometimes realized that I was no longer in agreement with my past thoughts. They had evolved, mutated— a person is a perpetual work in progress. I only kept the pages that had stood up to time. The others flew away on their own. Ungainly forms, stones would appear, but the streams kept flowing. While writing, ideas that had no connection to my topic would sometimes drift in and I took note of these outpourings. They would sometimes be clear as crystal, adorned with radiant words. Other times they were soiled, enveloped in amniotic fluid, premature and unformed. Then came periods of waiting, of giving the sap enough time to become milk. Then the work of revising, of choosing, of pruning, of refining, of percussion. I would hesitate over several words, I would choose one, make a note, then cross it out; I would be ruthless. It was a work of clarification, of making closer correspondences. An inner self-sculpture, an auto-clarification, locating my inner truth beneath the wooly layers, keeping track of inconsistencies and mimeses, finding words for what is essential. Sometimes the language confessed its inability to speak.

I strained to describe my states of consciousness, and at times the words did not manage to state the way things appeared to me, the way things happened or did not happen. Writing: a time of consciousness, a time tracking, a punctuation of the flow.

Death *cuts short* most human works. On that day, I switched off the ignition and parked the car in a lot. I decided to finish the book that I was reading. Finish reading as though to finish living. I stopped the passage of time. Now on familiar terms with the cosmos, the flow, the source, I discovered that nothing could prevent the completion of this instant (act). That's what eternity is—a quietude, a fullness, a completion. An act (instant) that time could no longer touch.

This text does not seal the work of my freedom. It is merely a conditioned response to my society, to my time, to the constraints it imposes upon me. Its writing bears witness not to my freedom, but to my aspiration for it. The only real evidence will be the lack of a need to write. For now, I content myself with its promises of clarity. Silence, perhaps, one day.

In the meantime, the jihad continues.

Translator's Notes

1 Captain Alexandre was the *nom de guerre* of French poet and WWII Resistance leader René Char. His work *Feuillets d'Hypnos* (*Leaves of Hypnos*) is widely considered one of the most significant works of 20th-century French poetry.

2 The *tisbaar* is the noon prayer (*Dhuhr*) in Islam, performed after the sun passes its zenith.

3 The Baye Fall are a prominent religious sect in Senegal whose members are known for their distinctive clothes and appearance. They are a branch group of the Mouride Sufi brotherhood.

4 The *salat* is the ritual prayer in Islam, performed five times daily by the faithful.

5 The *nafila* are supererogatory prayers often performed during Ramadan.

6 The *Fatiha* is the first Surah (chapter) of the Quran, known as "The Opening." It is recited at the beginning of every daily prayer.

7 The *Bismillah* is a foundational Islamic phrase meaning "In the name of God, the Most Gracious, the Most Merciful."

8 The *rakat* is a single cycle of movements and recitations within the salat.

9 The *tashahhud* is a litany recited while sitting at the conclusion of two rakats and at the end of the salat.